POVERTY

A VIOLATION
OF LAW

POVERTY

A VIOLATION
OF LAW

By

CHARLES W. GARNACHE

A SOCKDOLAGER

Gulf of Maine Publishing

ISBN 0-9667320-2-2

Gulf of Maine Publishing
P.O. Box 353
Biddeford Pool, ME   04006

Edited by Kathryn Garnache

Cover Photograph & Cover
Design by Kathryn Garnache

Printed in the United States of America.

DEDICATION

Kathy and Christina

And a special thanks to
Priscilla Kelley

CONTENTS

INTRODUCTION

The right appeals to us to save freedom by obeying the laws of God. The founders advised us to obey the "Laws of Nature and Nature's God".

When was the last time that anyone heard a politician advise anyone to obey the Laws of Nature? America is known as a land of laws. Unfortunately, far too many of our rules and regulations (laws) are based on the authority of our legislators and not on the authority of the "Laws of Nature and Nature's God". Often such laws are based on opinions and result in endless unforeseen consequences.

All manmade laws must first agree with Natural Law. The Laws of Nature have been in existence forever and take precedence over anything man can come up with; otherwise, a just law cannot be created. Laws that conflict with Nature are based on error and can only result in chaos, poverty, and tyranny.

It is the duty of the citizens of a free society to have basic knowledge of Natural Law; just as it is the duty of the physically able to defend the nation (self-defense) against those who would commit offensive aggression against its citizens.

This work is written so that the lay person can easily understand it. It is not intended to impress academia. I am not an academic. I am a self-educated lay person who is speaking to my fellow citizens. Academics find little, if anything, they can agree on as truth. Global warming is a case in point.

It is important to understand what I am saying here -- one should recognize the difference between economics as defined in Wikipedia as "the social science that studies the production, distribution, and consumption of goods and services". Whereas Natural Law Private Property economics deals with the citizen's right to life and freedom.

Because Industrial Economics is vital to one's earning income (private property) that is used to maintain his life, the difference between the two is of little consequence. When one is obedient to the dictates of Natural Law, he will respect the property of all others, including those for whom he works. When private property rights are damaged through the destructive actions of others, one has had his right to life infringed upon and his freedom damaged. If this happens often enough, the result is poverty and loss of freedom. The natural consequence of the loss of freedom is poverty.

In socialist nations, socialism is the number one subject in the school systems. In capitalist America, capitalism is seldom, if ever, mentioned in a positive way in our public schools. Also the subject of Natural Law is never mentioned in the schools or in the media. Even our law schools overlook Natural Law for the most part. Students attend public schools for twelve years so that they can go to the Department of Employment Security and register themselves as unskilled!

I am a veteran of World War II. I believe that the effort I am making at this time to be more important than dropping bombs from a B-24.

Our nation is on the path to socialism. Socialism is an economic system based on opinion, not Natural Law. Our only defense is to understand Natural Law Private Property Rights. This is the premise upon which this nation was founded. All have the right to life, liberty, and the pursuit of happiness under the [authority] of the "Laws of Nature and Nature's God".

There are those who believe America was founded on Judeo Christian principles, Bill O'Reilly, for instance. The founders were influenced to a considerable degree by Judeo Christian principles, but, as I just said, it is Natural Law Private Property Rights under the [authority] of the "Laws of Nature and Nature's God" that is the foundation of this nation.

The most important words ever written in the history of mankind are in our founding documents -- "...that all men have the right to, life, liberty and the pursuit of happiness..." "...And to assume among the Powers of the Earth, the separate and equal Station in which the Laws of Nature and Nature's God entitle them." (The Declaration of Independence.)

From these words in the Declaration of Independence only one conclusion can be drawn -- we are obliged to conduct ourselves in obedience to the "Laws of Nature and Nature's God" -- all else constitutes opinion. I capitalize Nature, just as I capitalize God, for the same reason.

The Moon

CHAPTER I

Nature's Laws took us to the moon -- violations will drive us to poverty.

Ａll will agree that we have the right to life. All generate income in order to maintain the life that God and Nature has given them. Taking some, or all, of one's income through legalized plunder (government) or illegal plunder (thieves, swindlers and Ponzi schemes) is in actual fact a denial of one's life to whatever degree one's income is taken from them. The responsibility is entirely that of governments everywhere on earth because a government's total responsibility is to protect its citizens from those who would act destructively against their fellow citizens. This includes, in particular, those within the government.

As people work to generate income to maintain their lives, they should work just as diligently to increase their knowledge of liberty so that all may live in freedom, prosperity, and justice.

When people cash their paychecks and look at the money in their hands, are they justified in believing that the money is theirs? If they use some of the money to buy tools, are they justified in believing that the newly purchased tools are their private property? Are the house and car that they have been paying on for years, their private property?

Not anymore! Actions by city councils, state governments, and the U.S. Supreme Court say no more! Whereas the Constitution empowers government to take private property for public use, in the case of *Kelo v. New London, Connecticut*, the court has given the town of New London the power to take private property for private use. By the use of eminent domain one's property now can go to the person, or persons, willing to redevelop the property to generate higher revenue.

In the town of Sanford, Maine, an old mill complex had been seized from the owner and transferred to a private group to be developed into a mall. The owner is to be paid one hundred fifty thousand dollars. This is a fraction of the actual worth of the land alone. The many large buildings are worth as much, if not more than the land. This real estate is in the center of the town. One acre in this location is worth more than one million dollars

With the power of eminent domain, property can be taken, but government must pay just compensation. Of course it is the government that determines what constitutes just compensation.

There are several ways that property can be taken with no compensation. If a so-called "endangered species" is found on private property, the property cannot be developed or used for any purpose. If there is a puddle on a piece of property, the Corps of Engineers can declare it a wetland after which it cannot be used. The owner of the land does not get any compensation.

*****

Capitalism is the only economic system based on Natural Law Private Property Rights that results in justice for all. It is my opinion that the environmentalists and organizations like the ACLU are anti-capitalists first, and nothing else, second. Justice is offensive to them. They will do all that is in their power to bring America under the rule of man and away from the rule of "Nature and Nature's God".

*****

I can sit with a group of my friends and discuss the problems of the day. We can go on for hours. We can come up with a consensus, a solution for health care, education, energy, whatever. When we are done, we all go on our merry way. Maybe we are better informed at the conclusion of our gabfest or what is more likely, more confused.

On the other hand, a group of legislators doing the same thing, walk away from their session leaving us with a new "law" or "regulation" based on their [opinions]. Occasionally we will end up with a good law. However, for the most part, we will realize a loss of another fragment of our freedom.

It is important to recognize that liberty and freedom, under certain circumstances, are different. A lawyer summarizing a case before a jury has freedom of speech, but he also has the liberty to speak. The judge has the liberty to interrupt the lawyer. Although the jurors maintain their freedom of speech and all the others in the courtroom have freedom of speech; they do not have the liberty to speak. If they take the liberty to speak, they will be ejected from the courtroom.

Today every outrage imaginable is defended under the misguided belief that slander, libel, and treason are protected by the first amendment. The first amendment never was intended to give citizens the freedom to commit treason, as Jane Fonda did during the Vietnam War; nor aid and comfort to the enemy that has become commonplace today in the war against terrorism.

People who are trusted to contribute to the security of our nation leak classified material. After all, they have freedom of speech. They do not have the liberty to compromise our nation's defenses, nor to endanger our troops and civilian workers in a war zone!

The executive branch of our government has to brief members of congress on the most sensitive matters that affect our national security. When one considers that the motivation of the members of congress is purely political, it becomes obvious that the most sensitive material is going to be leaked. Even people in the FBI and the CIA, who have a political ax to grind, are going to leak secret documents.

"Everyone wants to save the world, but no one will help mama with the dishes!" In other words, if one wishes to improve humanity, he should start by working on himself. If one would reform himself by even a microscopic part, the world would be better by that amount. Multiply that by a few million times and one might even be able to notice the difference. "Hey! The old neighborhood does not look that bad after all!"

How did we get into this mess? Every day thousands upon thousands of people are killed. The killers for the most part are governments. It is their job to prevent killing, and yet they are the worst culprits. Millions upon millions of people are plundered every day. The plunderers are governments all over the world. It's supposed to be their job to prevent plunder. Rather than stop it, they have legalized it. Now we have legalized plunder!

America is the world's number one super power. It cannot, or refuses to, seal its borders. As Dr. Phil would ask, "And how is that working for you?" If sealing our borders is not job one for the military, then what is? If our borders were properly sealed, we wouldn't have to worry about terrorists doing us harm. They wouldn't be here to begin with. But as it is, between Muslims and Mexicans, we have twenty million potential mischief-makers in our midst. In the past people migrated to America to become Americans. The Mexicans and Muslims have no intention to assimilate. On the first day that the Mexicans protested immigration laws, what flag were they carrying? "The American flag was noticeable by its absence." By the next day the protesters realized that not displaying the American flag was a PR disaster. Now they featured the American flag along with their own Mexican flag.

*****

It is the great increase in productivity that has prevented the bankrupting of western economics. The blue-collar worker provides all with food, clothing, and shelter. There is a great need for white-collar workers -- the city hall workers, schoolteachers, clerks of all kinds, etc. The blue collars produce the goods that keep us alive.

NAFTA was supposed to cause a great "sucking sound of American jobs going south". The great sucking

sounds were people moving north to fill the need for
workers. The truth of the matter is that we had jobs for
twenty million aliens. Unemployment stood at four
points. It is seven percent at this writing and heading to
ten percent. Five percent is considered full employment.
Five percent represents the people in transit from one job
to another. The Obama presidency is going to be a
textbook demonstration of the government's creating
poverty

It is corporate America that provides the blue
collars with jobs that result in growing wealth for all. It is
impossible to help the wage earner by harming the wage
payer.

It is corporate America that pays the wages of
every politician in the local, state, and central
governments. Corporate America indirectly pays the
wages of every cop, firefighter, schoolteacher, sanitation
worker, street sweeper, military person, etc.

Enron was not a failure of corporate America. It
was a failure of government whose job it is to protect its
citizens from predators. Madoff's fifty-billion-dollar
Ponzi scheme and the bursting of the housing bubble were
failures of government, not failures of the private sector.

When corporations act destructively toward
workers and stockholders, it is a failure of government,
not the free market. The result is a loss of freedom and
quality of life. It is the government's responsibility to
maintain order. Capitalists cannot use force to maintain
order. It is not their job. The use of force by
entrepreneurs is against the law

Governments use force to "stop or fend off those
who act destructively" -- (Leonard Reed, THE
FOUNDATION FOR ECONOMIC EDUCATION) --
when they are limited to functions within the authority

given to them by the people. Governments cannot exercise any rights that were not first held by the citizens under the authority of Nature. People existed before governments; therefore, rights advance from the citizens to the government, not from the government to the nation.

How can we survive as a free nation when the majority of citizens are illiterate as to how freedom works? One third of Americans have no idea where government gets its money. One third believes government has its own money, and one third are painfully aware that government gets its money from them! (Conclusions of endless polls.)

Of what I have written so far one can believe it, or not. It is one's choice, but one can be sure that deer, dogs, cats, squirrels, chipmunks, and all of the creatures of the seas and the sky, never needed to have this sort of discussion. The only laws governing their activities are the Laws of Nature. They have no choice. They must obey because they have to act according to their instincts

Humans are cursed with a brain that enables them to justify anything and everything they do. It depends on "whose ox is being gored".

The human brain is corrupt. The brains of all other living creatures are as pure as Nature. They do not wage wars, kill for the fun of it, or do anything that is not in harmony with their nature. Humans violate their nature in every possible way one can imagine. We are a paradox, constantly fighting ourselves. We tear ourselves apart within and are belligerent to the point of inflicting harm on others. On the other side of this monster we call human, are those who dedicate their lives to the service of others. Humans are this way because they have freewill. They can choose to be good, or to be evil. Humans make up governments everywhere. Can anyone deny that politicians are like a swarm of mosquitoes that drives us to distraction?

*****

The purest culture that ever existed on planet earth are the members of the First Nations -- what Columbus called Indians, and others refer to as native Americans.

All citizens born in America are native Americans, but are not members of the First Nation or the First People.

The First Nation was pure. Like the bear, wolf, and other creatures, they marked their territory and fought to protect it from trespassers. They never invaded their neighboring Nation for the purpose of taking their territory and subjecting its members to the invaders' rules. They did, on occasion, raid their neighbors and take some of their women. The more women they had the better their chances were to survive as a nation. This is as close as the First Nations came to offensive violence.

The First Nation lived close to Nature. They obeyed Nature's Laws. Therefore they limited themselves to acts of self-defense. Defensive violence is imposed on us by Nature. Offensive violence is a violation of the Laws of Nature.

The First Nation saw everything through the Laws of Nature. This contributed mightily to their wisdom. Their children were never disciplined. They became responsible adults by copying the behavior of their parents. (Pride Publications, Inc., 22 Emerson St., Wakefield, Mass.)

Americans, for the most part, would like to see all of the nations of the world have a democratic form of government. Even if this were possible, democracy would die within one or two generations. It is freedom that we should strive to expand. If we were successful in spreading freedom and the knowledge of freedom, democracy would follow.

How can people who have never known freedom maintain a democracy? In America, with hundreds of years of freedom, only about one in four citizens can be considered politically literate. If one doesn't think so, then think about this -- in the next national election only half of those who are eligible will vote. The other half do not want to support those they consider to be self-serving politicians. That means that of the remaining fifty percent, a little more than half will determine who will be the next minority candidate to become president of the United States.

Furthermore, the United States is being invaded by millions of unarmed illegal immigrants who are not coming here to become Americans like immigrants of the past, but to change America into the image of serfdom from which they came.

*****

Obedience to the Laws of Nature made it possible to put persons on the moon. The laws of engineering are actually Laws of Nature. The laws of economics fall under the Laws of Nature. Whatever one sees or does falls within Natural Law. Scientists who searched for unknown truths discovered all the laws necessary to build the space shuttle. They were not free to alter a single principle. They were not free to substitute opinion for law. If they had, their efforts would have failed. On the path of discovery, failures occur. Scientists learn from their failures and incorporate their newfound knowledge, which results in a better machine.

From the Wright Brothers to the modern airliner, an endless chain of discovery of Natural Law principles brought the miracle of modern aviation to fruition. From Henry Ford's Model T to the modern luxury cars, the same holds true. The trading of a loaf of bread has to be accomplished within the dictates of Nature's Laws.

When one distinguishes between Natural Law Private Property economics and industrial economics, one could almost conclude that the difference is more like splitting hairs than finding a meaningful difference.

No one would try to build anything without having to obey the dictatorship of Nature. Freedom depends on total compliance to the first precept of Natural Law and the Commandments. From the Commandment, "Thou shalt not kill", and the first precept of Natural Law, "self-survival", (Thomas Aquinas), we come to a universal truth that each individual has a right to life.

It follows logically and within reason, if we have the right to life then we have the right to those things necessary to sustain that life. Those things are the fruits of our labor. (Not someone else's labor.) The fruits of our labor constitute our private property. Being our property we are free to exchange it with anyone for his or her property of comparable value if the exchange is free of compulsion. This is what is called capitalism!

All have a right to life. One generates income in order to maintain his right to life. Any taking of the individual's income generated by legalized plunder (government) or illegal plunders (thieves, scam artists, price fixing, Ponzi schemes) are, in actual fact, denying one's right to life to whatever degree that his income is taken from him. This cannot be said too often.

Freedom and prosperity cannot survive without strict and uncompromising adherence to private property rights. For most of history, Americans' private property rights were jealously guarded. Unfortunately, the Supreme Court ruled that the power of eminent domain could be used to take the property of private individuals and transfer it to others, or to corporations. However, they would have to destroy the homes on the property and replace them with construction that would return higher taxes to the community -- *Kelo v. City of New London.*

Today, all of the homes have been destroyed, and the developers have decided not to build!

There is no end to private land being shut down to any form of development without compensation to the owners. In my community, if an individual who owned an apartment building wished to convert it to condos, he must give the present tenants the equivalent of two months' rent. You can be sure if that part of the ordinance made it mandatory for council members to pay the two months' rent out of their own pockets, it never would have passed.

One can measure the prosperity of a nation by the degree that property rights are respected. Switzerland, Taiwan, and Hong Kong are three of the most prosperous nations on earth. They protect property rights enthusiastically. In contrast, there are no property rights in Cuba or North Korea. These and most of Africa are the poorest nations on earth. The closer a nation comes to one-man rule, the poorer that nation becomes. China, on the other hand, has an economy where property rights are expanding rapidly and so is wealth. Greater freedom is sure to follow.

If a person's home were burglarized, that person would be poorer because of it. If one were robbed on the street, that person would be poorer for their property would have been taken from them. If government taxed its citizens excessively, they would be poorer as the government would have what was theirs. The denial or taking of one's property is a violation of Natural Law and promotes poverty.

Taxes are the chief means of taking property (income from one's labor); consequently, the chief means of creating poverty. President Johnson's "War on Poverty" created poverty. All one has to do to prove that point is to do the math. There are more people who live under the poverty level today than ever. This happened in spite of full employment, record wages and trillions spent to end poverty. Obama is about to demonstrate the power of government to create poverty.

Each time wages go up by a percentage point, great numbers of workers find themselves in a higher tax bracket. More money equals less purchasing power. If one gets the impression that congress's goal is to find new ways to extract money from the citizenry, they would be right. On the local level, fees are the new cash cow. What used to cost a few dollars, now costs in the thousands. Building permits are a good example.

These are but a few examples as to what is happening. As the taxman takes more and more of the private sector money, the poorer everybody becomes. Our salvation is that worker productivity outpaces the tax collector. How long can the private sector keep ahead of the government's greed? Not much longer if citizens cannot make the connection that taxes constitute the taking of private property.

In the private sector greed is a virtue if government does its job and limits corporations to gaining wealth by providing quality goods and services. There is no restriction on greed within the government. The government polices the private sector. Who polices the government?

Of course government has to have money to function. Washington and the Supreme Court have expanded their power way beyond what is allowed by the Constitution.

Section 8 of the Constitution itemizes the power of the central government in plain, understandable English that any layman of normal intelligence can easily understand. It gets confusing when members of the intelligencia, while practicing the art of mental gymnastics, seek to hide what the Constitution says in a fog of double think.

Amendment IX says the enumeration in the Constitution of certain rights shall not be construed to deny or disparage others retained by the people. Amendment X states that "The powers not delegated to the United States by the Constitution, nor prohibited by it to the states ARE RESERVED TO THE STATES RESPECTIVELY, OR TO THE PEOPLE."

The only way to reverse this trend is through education. Do not look at public or higher education. This is where capitalism is shredded and the public sector (socialism) is advanced as the savior of humanity.

As capitalism is taxed in more and diverse ways from the hotdog stand to major corporations, and the minimum wage rises, poverty will expand. The teenager will find it more difficult to find work, and employers will be reluctant to hire. This corrupting means of taking property must be recognized as a violation of Natural Law and the creator of poverty. Like a thief in the night, the government's plundering of private property by stealth is hardly noticeable. As theft is institutionalized by government actions, morality of the nation deteriorates.

The word capitalism is seldom used in the media. I don't recall the last time, if ever, I saw a reference to Natural Law. There are many euphemisms used to describe capitalists -- the rich, the winners of life's lottery, the privileged, the upper class, the upper crust. Capitalists are people, from the paperboy to Bill Gates, who make money by selling products and services. They are the very people who have brought us the wonders of today's world.

Capitalism is the mother of freedom, the salvation of the poor, the servant of morality and Nature's Laws. It is private property's guardian angel. Capitalism created the computer that I am working on. I can hear the washer and dryer in the background, the result of capitalism. Everywhere I look I see the benefits of capitalism -- the house I live in, the vehicles in my drive, UPS, my TV, food, clothing, etc. This is wealth. Everywhere I look I see some of that wealth being siphoned off by taxes. Wealth creates wealth. After taxes there is less wealth to create wealth, ergo, taxes promote poverty. An austere government will have little harmful effect on the creation of wealth. The more interventionist government becomes, the more destructive it is to the creation of wealth.

Nature's Rule vs. Man

CHAPTER II

Thomas Paine had a clear vision of Nature. He saw the wonders of planet earth. He recognized our most valuable resources -- air, water, and grass. He looked out at the vastness of space and wondered how many other planets similar to ours could be out there? As he marveled at the beauty, power, and perfection all around him; he saw God.

Nature and all living things are perfect, no flaws, except man whose mind is corrupt. Humans evolved; and in the process of evolution, the most cunning survived to produce the next generation. The question arises, "Do we have freewill, or are we just cunning?"

Are humans shrewd, crafty, ingenious, pleasing, charming, and skilled in deception and guile? They are all of these things; therefore, it is right to conclude that humans are cunning. Other creatures possess many of these qualities, but they do not behave in a destructive way. They are not free to violate their Nature, even though many are as cunning as are humans. Man can act destructively because he is free to violate Nature's laws; therefore, it is right to conclude that humans have freewill.

Eventually, freewill that is driven by superstition and greed could result in the destruction of the human species. Most humans limit themselves to being creative; therefore, it is conceivable that good will triumph over evil.

The creators of poverty, governments, spend all of their time devising ways to separate citizens from their property. If an act of the city council, state legislature, or the federal government costs an individual money, then he now has less to spend on himself. He is poorer than before the act became law. Even worse, another little piece of his freedom has been chipped away. As the fruit of one's labor is taken, so is a corresponding amount of one's freedom.

If one went for a walk in the forest, he would soon hear the shrieking call of the blue jay that would warn every creature within hearing distance of its call that human trespassers have entered their space. It also makes a much more subdued guttural sound when things are safe. Chipmunks would sit upright on a stone wall to warn its extended family that a hawk was gliding overhead. Seagulls would scream to let other gulls know that they have found a source of food. A deer would make a subdued hush to warn other deer that danger is near. A cat purrs when it is contented. Humans talk, and talk without end, quite often several at a time. In Maine it is said, "If it doesn't improve on silence, it is best left unsaid." I do not think that Mainers pay much attention to their own wisdom. I am hearing-impaired. Sometimes I have to ask my wife to repeat herself several times. She will say with a voice full of frustration, "You are making me waste my words!" The human voice is a thing of beauty -- a mother cooing to her baby; a voice raised in song, the sound of a full choir.

Our fellow creatures have a sound to warn each other of impending danger and, for the most part, another subdued sound when they are contented. The different sounds they make cannot be confused. There was a time that when a person was talking, others in the group would listen. Each one would speak without being interrupted or having others talk at the same time. Not anymore; now everybody talks at the same time. Unlike the creatures of the wild, the net result of the detonation of sounds is confusion, controversy, and a lack of credibility on the part of the participants. Nowhere is this more obvious than in the halls of congress. All of the talk has a political objective. Senators call for an investigation of the oil companies and charge price gouging. The oil companies have a margin of pennies per gallon. The government collects over forty cents a gallon, and congress is considering adding two dollars more per gallon! It is a rare member of congress who would mention the fact that if there were price gouging going on, the culprit would be the government. This is another example of how government creates poverty.

Legislators pass new laws. Citizens soon find loopholes in those laws. Legislators then pass laws to plug the loopholes. Individuals then find two holes in the laws intended to close the original loopholes. Next come regulations, rules, amendments, and court actions. The original intent of the legislation had not been met, nor will it ever. By then the political mosquitoes have drained the blood from their intended victim. Another industry was on the verge of collapse.

The northeast American lobster fishery is the healthiest fishery in the world. Every year the previous year's record is broken, if not in actual numbers of lobsters caught, then in the money value of the catch. There is an army of fishcrats determined to prevent the collapse of this fishery; however, they cannot provide a shred of evidence that a collapse is possible. In fact, there is solid evidence that the coming season is going to be another record breaker. This does not stop the mosquitoes from working overtime to damage this bastion of capitalism and individualism, and they are succeeding. The lobster fishery is now in decline.

In the name of protecting the right whale from extinction, the lobstermen have been forced to modify their fishing gear at the cost to the industry of millions of dollars. Lobstermen from young pups to persons pushing ninety have never seen a right whale in the area where they fish for lobsters. There is one exception, the area near Mt. Desert Island, Maine. The right whale travels from Cape Cod to the Gulf of St. Lawrence. No one seems to know what route that they take to get there. For all that the scientists know, they could go to Canada by way of the English Channel.

The right whale is a candidate for the dumbest animal on land or water. Large cargo vessels cause most of their fatalities. This animal is not smart enough to get out of the way of slow-moving coastal ships. The humpback and mink whales are around commercial fishing vessels and their gear all of the time with little, if any, provable evidence of injury or death caused by the fishermen.

The greens fight to protect the endangered species while, at the same time, they work toward the extinction of invasive species. If it is a kangaroo rat discovered on the farmer's land, the farmer loses the use of his land. If it is an Asian shore crab, kill it! It is not on the list of endangered species, but is on the list of species that pose a threat to others. (www.vitalsignsme.org)

What environmental god determines which species will live and which ones will be exterminated? Isn't this a choice that Hitler made with humans whom he considered not worthy of life?

Lobster traps are set in trawls from three traps to thirty, some even more, depending on the size of the vessel. The pot warp (rope) that connects everything from the buoy to the lead trap is comprised of float rope and sink rope. Float rope is used between all the traps and twenty fathoms or more, depending on the depth, on the line leading to the buoy. From the float rope, sink rope is used up to the buoy. The float rope is used to keep the line off the bottom and prevent chafing and the loss of traps. It also prevents the line from being tangled on the hard bottom. If the line is hung down on the bottom, the trawl is lost. To replace the trawl would cost about eighty dollars per trap. Sink rope is used from the buoy to the float line. This prevents exposing any line on the surface where it could be cut off by passing vessels.

The way trawls were rigged in the past, this was an annoying problem, but not a bankroll buster. By regulation (law) starting in 2008, all trawls must be rigged with sink or neutral-buoyant rope. (Neutral buoyant? What the hell is that?) The sink rope between traps will cause endless problems, as the rope keeps getting hung down and chaffing off. This regulation will bankrupt many families' fishing businesses with more government-promoted poverty, and more families will fall prey to the anti-capitalist greens. By the way, has anyone seen a family farm lately?

It has taken years to bring about these regulations. The nature of government is to stop or fend off;

consequently, it moves at a snail's pace. The capitalist makes a decision one-day, and implements it the next.

What about Natural Law? Does it have five layers of bureaucracy before it can react? No. Does Nature have to meet in huge chambers populated by individuals whose consciences were traded in years before for votes? No. Does it have to get the approval of committees? No. Does it have to pass its decision to bureaus for enforcement? No. Most important of all, does its laws create poverty or wealth?

If Natural Law were obeyed to the letter, there would be no infringement of property rights. If governments enforced laws that harmonized with the Laws of Nature, they would then promote wealth. When all workers are allowed to keep a fair share of their earnings, they will be invigorated to increase their productivity. With inspired energy they will increase their welfare by converting natural resources to usable products by the use of tools.

With governments acting in honorable ways, this will influence citizens to become more respectful. In most elections less than fifty percent of the eligible voters participate. This means that a minority of twenty-five percent determines the members of government. This is considered disgraceful. It is said that if you don't vote, you have nothing to complain about. Well, what if fifty percent of the voters considered their choice to be between Tweedledee and Tweedledum? In that case they would consider them all to be unworthy!

The late Leonard Read, founder of the FOUNDATION FOR ECONOMIC EDUCATION, argued that one has a third choice when he goes to the polls. If one believed that a vote for either candidate would be a vote for the lesser of two evils, then he should leave that portion of the ballot blank. He argued that when thousands upon thousands of ballots would come in blank, this would encourage better-qualified candidates to seek election.

*****

Natural Law is complete. There are vast unknown aspects of Nature yet to be discovered. Scientists will continue to discover laws pertaining to the human body and mind. Scientific discovery will make it possible to build machines that we cannot even imagine. OPEC will be left with their oil in the ground, just as the coal miners priced themselves out of the market.

Each discovery of Nature equals perfect truth. Each new law out of congress is full of holes. Unlike Nature's Laws that solve problems, congress creates laws that are problems. Nature's Laws are the foundation that property rights rest upon. Congressional laws are opinions, like the termites that eat away at the foundation of property rights.

Wealth is created by labor that converts natural resources with the use of tools into usable products. If there were no natural resources to convert into products, then wealth could not be created.

The greens have destroyed the northwest lumber industry on the pretense that the endangered spotted owl was threatened. The New England fishing industry is being destroyed on the pretense that it endangers the right whale.

We are not permitted to drill for oil in many places with known large deposits of oil on the pretense that the environment would be damaged. We are denied permission to drill in areas of the Gulf of Mexico, but the

Communist Chinese can! Land with a puddle on it cannot be developed because the puddle constitutes a wetland.

One can only conclude that environmental opinions are anti-capitalist and, therefore, anti property rights. Under the subterfuge of protecting Nature, they are violating the Laws of Nature by creating poverty. Ask the New England fishermen, the northwest lumbermen, and the roughneck who is out of work because of the enviros. Ask them how prosperous they felt after the banks foreclosed on their property because the area from which they drew their income had been declared off-limits. With their way of life gone, they must now enter a world where they feel they do not belong

Not only does the political interventionist cause financial harm, the psychological damage is unknown and beyond measure. The culture (nation) that was part of their spirit and their soul, is now gone.

The same can be said about the family farms and the hundreds of family fishing businesses. Family logging enterprises are feeling the same pain.

The enforcers of government laws carry guns. You obey the law, or they will kill you! No way, one would argue. Every way, I argue. A recent Supreme Court ruling allowed the taking of private property through Eminent Domain to be transferred to others. The new owners would be obliged to develop the property in order to create greater revenue for the community. If the evicted person refused to vacate his property, the force of law would be brought in to evict him. The property owner would resist the force brought to bear to evict him by the use of his own force. To leave the property, the owner would be agreeing to the injustice that he opposed. He has determined that he will not yield in any way. As the police effort mounts to break the stand off, the resistance by the citizen accelerates to a corresponding degree. He is armed. He is determined that he is not going to surrender what has been his home for all of his life for the benefit of a big-box store. From that point it is an argument as to who fired first. In any event, the person is dead, lying on the floor that he had walked on all of his life, with his babies and with his spouse. They are now all gone.

Construction on the big-box store will begin on time. The grand opening will also be on time. They have their lawyers; and the property owners have their loose change.

Nature does not tolerate violation of its laws. Property rights have been violated. The punishment? Another chip cut from the granite of freedom.

Organized Force

CHAPTER III

Government is organized force. It has an Army, Navy, Marine Corps, and Air Force, Coast Guard, CIA, FBI, and several other agencies, all of which carry guns. On the local level they have the National Guard, State Police, Sheriff's Department, and the local Police Department. All of these carry guns. A gun is used to subdue someone or to kill him or her. Those who enforce laws and government mandates also use their guns to protect themselves.

If a nation's police forces were used to enforce laws that were in harmony with the laws of Nature, then they would be limited to act against people who committed offensive violence, i.e., who acted destructively.

Government is force -- compulsion -- and when this force is used in harmony with the laws of Nature, a nation enjoys property rights and freedom. When government force does violence to Natural Law principles, there is no freedom. With freedom denied, what is left is force. This force now becomes offensive violence and destructive. James A. Donald wrote in

Natural Law and Natural Rights, "A ruler that violates natural law is illegitimate. He has no right to be obeyed; his commands are mere force and coercion. Rulers who act lawlessly, whose laws are unlawful, are criminals, and should be dealt with in accordance with Natural Law, as applied in a state of nature, in other words they and their servants should be killed as the opportunity presents, like the dangerous animals that they are, the common enemies of all mankind."

He goes on to say, "John Locke's writings were a call to arms, an assertion of the right and duty to forcibly remove illegitimate rulers and their servants. This provided the moral and legal basis for many great revolutions, and many governments. After the American Revolution the North Americans were governed more or less in accordance with Natural Law for one hundred and thirty years."

It is sad to see the great American nation descend into a state of lawlessness where not only the Constitution but also the laws of Nature (Natural Law takes precedence over the Constitution) are being violated on a daily basis. As the central government becomes more corrupt, the state and local governments follow suit, along with their citizens. Growing poverty is a natural consequence.

When people are paid for their labor, they feel great. When they see the amount of their earnings kept out of their paychecks, they feel as if they have been mugged. When one considers the near-total ignorance of Natural Law principles everywhere in the world today, the worker should feel like he has been deprived.

Laypersons are not expected to be experts on the subject of Natural Law, although it would be to their great benefit if they were. Politicians should be required to be experts in this area. How can they promote just laws if they are unfamiliar with Natural Law? It is to the police that the burden and responsibility of being informed falls the heaviest. The difference between Hitler's Germany and the United States is its police force. Without the support of the German police forces, Hitler could not have driven Europe to poverty. Without the work of the American police forces, our present level of wealth would not have been possible because they are the protectors of property.

Before there were governments (police forces), there was Natural Law. There were people who had property and rights under the authority of Nature. Government cannot have rights that are not first held by the people because the people were here first. Governments cannot interfere with private property rights because private property rights existed before governments. Governments get their authority from the people.

James Donald, Thomas Paine, John Locke, Adam Smith, Leonard Read, and others advocated that a ruler who was in violation of Natural Law was a dangerous criminal; and he and all those who served him should be killed. We have not reached that extreme in America as yet. The democratic process is still working for the time being. The citizens, educated on the subject of Natural Law, if in the majority, could change the direction of the nation. Our present prosperity is due to the seeds of a hundred and fifty years of being governed by laws agreeable to Nature. Private property violations are in their infancy, so we do not feel the effects at the moment. Government is organized force, but the electorate is a more powerful force in a democratic society. Armed with primary knowledge (which is the knowledge being articulated here), the American nation can survive two hundred years and more.

America is at greater risk than ever before in its history. The greatest threat is the invasion from Mexico. Like the threat from the Muslims, the Mexican invaders are not organized into military units. They cross our borders with impunity. They do not carry weapons or wear uniforms. They come here to work. In a few years they will constitute the largest voting block in the country. Then the face of America will have a definite Spanish look. We have corruption now. A Mexican United States will be undistinguishable from Mexico of today, as corrupt as a nation can become.

Without firing a shot America, will fall to the Mexicans. They know nothing about our Constitution or private property rights (capitalism). With them in charge, government mosquitoes will become hornets.

Mexico's poverty and corruption are due to the lack of Natural rights for its citizens. James A. Donald defines it this way, "Natural law and natural rights follow from the Nature of man and the world. We have the right to defend our property and ourselves, because of the kind of animal we are. True law derives from this right, not from the arbitrary power of the omnipotent state."

Because a Natural Law and natural right is denied Mexicans, the government is criminal and should be done away with just as the American colonists did away with British rule. At that time there were many Americans familiar with Natural Law. Mexico does not have the equivalent moral force. A person knows in their gut that what they earn is theirs. Mexicans do not possess the skill or knowledge to bring about the change of government based on Natural Law.

There are those in America who argue for a "living constitution" -- one that keeps up with the changing and progressing times. They are wrong! The American Constitution is based on Natural Law and is as relevant today as it was when ratified two hundred years ago. It will be as relevant two thousand years from now as it is today. Nature does not change. As study finds unknown laws of Nature, this does not make what we know today obsolete. As technology advances it does not make Natural Law obsolete, in fact it proves it to be immutable.

There can be no justice, no prosperity without the protection of private property. This is Mexico's problem and the problem of nations everywhere in the world that function as Mexico does.

It is sad to say that America has started down the road traveled by all the poverty-ridden countries in the world. A short while ago I could go to the county court house, research the deed to my home and prove it was mine. No one could take it from me. Not anymore, my home sets a half-mile inland from the beaches of the Gulf of Maine. Developers, who have ingratiated themselves with the local powers that be, a few years from now, will look at my land and my neighbor's land. Our land will be taken from us by the cities' power of Eminent Domain, and our homes will be replaced by high-rise condos. From these buildings the view of the Atlantic Ocean will be breath taking. Now I cannot even see the ocean. Large oak, maple and birch trees block the view. But I can hear the surf when I am out in my yard or in my bed at night. I have no visible neighbors. I am buried in the forest. My front yard is a private zoo where every creature that lives in this part of Maine visits every day. My home does not deface the side of a mountain or the shoreline. It is not visible from the highway or even from my nearest neighbor's house. I live in the bosom of Nature; it is paradise, a heaven on earth. No, it is not for sale!

We do have mosquitoes and in May, black flies. A black fly will give one an itch equal to the mosquito, but they will draw blood and the itch lasts for days. They are such pests; they will drive moose out of the forest. A good dose of *OFF* will keep them away. Oh, if it were that easy to drive the political mosquitoes away. Knowledge of Natural Law is the insect repellent *OFF*! It is the only tool we have to maintain our property rights.

With a government as powerful as ours, it is vital that power be used within the limits of Natural Law. The organized force that is government maintains a military to protect our nation against predator nations. The job of the military is to kill people and break things, like cities and the like.

In WWII I was a crewmember on a B-24. We dropped our bombs. We did not see the death and destruction we caused. If we were hit and went down, we would have all died together. Unlike the foot soldier who saw his best buddy blown away and then grieved the rest of his life, we had no time to grieve for each other. It all happened too quickly. If we were never hit, we lived with the horror of seeing our friends die. For the rest of our lives, we would never sleep in peace. Teenagers and boys in their early twenties would never know a day of peace, ever!

What is a just war? How can war be justified under any circumstances? My father argued that if the leaders of two nations ready to go to war were armed, then locked in a stadium and allowed to shoot it out amongst themselves, there would never be another war!

Offensive Violence

CHAPTER IV

This part of the discussion is limited to acts of humans toward each other. The violence that occurs between all of the other creatures is brought about in their attempts to feed themselves and secure their territory from encroachment. Much of the violence between humans is an attempt to take the property of others upon which their lives depend.

As human violence escalates between nations, the longer the conflict goes on, the more complex it is to determine who "threw the first punch". There is no argument that an act of self-defense is justified. The controversy begins when one tries to determine who is defending himself and his property.

The Japanese attack on Pearl Harbor was clearly an act of offensive violence. America's actions in Iraq are not as clearly defined. 9/11 cost more American lives than Pearl Harbor. The Japanese carried out Pearl Harbor. The Muslims carried out 9/11.

America went after the Japanese wherever they were and we should go after the radical Muslims wherever they are. 9/11 was an act of offensive violence. Nature dictates an individual or a nation must act in self-defense. The individual is part of a nation and has the natural right of self-defense; therefore, the nation derives its rights from the individual. Nations are people. Their country is the real estate they live upon. One cannot travel across a nation, only the country the nation occupies.

Hate, or the desire to take a nation's property, can drive offensive aggression. The radical Muslims are driven by hate of Americans. They argue that their hate is justified because of the crimes Christians have committed against the Muslim world, and all infidels should be killed.

Eric Fromm defines hate as rational and irrational. To hate someone because of their ethnicity or the color of their skin or any similar non-threatening reason is irrational hate. To hate someone because they pose a threat to one's wellbeing, such as a supervisor who tries to drive one out of his job, is rational hate. Under this definition it is right to conclude that the Muslims' hate of Americans is irrational hate. Prior to 9/11 America was no threat to the Arab world. Here we see how there is a vast difference of opinion. Is there a difference of opinion when one claims to have a right to life? The answer is no, because here we are stating a truth based on Natural Law.

Poverty is a violation of Natural Law. Considering that truth, one can predict with certainty that the governments of Bolivia and Venezuela are the next two nations to sink into poverty. With the confiscation of private property as a stated goal of the government, first foreign investment will cease. Next unemployment will rise, followed by the inflated price of a 1955 Chevrolet, the trademark of Cuban-style poverty. And somehow, through the use of tortured logic, Americans will be blamed. Is it any wonder that I conclude that the human mind is Nature's practical joke? The greater the ignorance of the people, the greater the opportunity for demagogues. They can manipulate the masses to believe their misery is everybody's fault but there own. By permitting the rulers to violate property rights, they have allowed the destruction of their economy. What are people to do against a government with a well-armed military?

They can do what the American colonist did. Poorly armed, if armed at all, they took on the most powerful nation on earth at that time and beat them.

The number one problem in the USA as I write this book is the cost of gasoline. The greens pressure congress to prevent drilling in the Gulf of Mexico, on Federal land which now constitutes a large part of the American landscape, and most importantly, in ANWR. The Arctic National Wildlife Refuge is bigger than most states. The drilling complex would be the size of a couple city blocks. One would need a global-positioning satellite to find a drilling operation, if one knew the coordinates. We now know that wildlife thrives along the pipelines and pumping stations of the great Alaskan pipeline. So it would not affect the caribou, white fox or any other creature; and I'm sure as hell not about to go visiting up there, nor is anyone else I know.

It's like northern Maine -- hundreds of thousands of acres where no roads or motorized machines are allowed. The idea is so people can enjoy the pristine beauty of this unspoiled wilderness. Sounds good. So how is anybody going to get there to enjoy it? It certainly will not be me with my arthritis and bad feet. I wonder if seaplanes are allowed to land on its ponds and lakes? Should one be able to get to one of the streams, ponds and lakes, would it be a permitted use if one were to try to get some fish? Oh, yes! Do not forget you're OFF! The human mosquitoes ordained this area, so one can bet they will be there in abundance. Are the Forest Rangers going to patrol this vast wilderness on foot? They can't do it by plane or helicopter, such noise pollution can't be allowed.

This is another example of property rights violations. Individuals singularly or in organized groups have the right to private property. Government is organized force whose authority emanates from its citizens. It has the responsibility to protect property; it does not have the right to private property.

"Wait a minute!" I am told, "government has all kinds of property."

"Sure they do."

"And how did they get it?"

"They bought it."

"With what?"

"With government money."

"And where did the government get its money?"

"Well, from the taxpayers, of course."

"Right. So what you call government property is actually the property of the tax-paying public. In other words, private property."

Every act that infringes, restricts, or limits property rights is a denial of human rights. There are many who will argue that human rights take precedence over property rights. They argue that the two are distinctive, one from the other. Property, as such, does not have rights. The owner of property has rights. Therefore, to say human rights take precedent over property rights is a fallacy. Private property rights and human rights are one and the same. One cannot have human rights without property rights.

Every problem must be viewed as a property rights problem. The ACLU is primarily an anti-capitalist organization. It attacks property rights through the subterfuge that it is battling those who would violate the First Amendment prohibition establishing the separation of church and state. It sues communities to force them to remove any reference to the Commandments. The Commandments, along with the first precept of Natural Law, establish our right to life. It is our right to life that establishes our right to private property. These truths are self-evident as stated in the Declaration of Independence. It cannot be said enough, we have a right to life. This is the basic premise upon which capitalism rests. It is a correct premise; consequently, everything that stems from it is correct, especially our right to property. Any opinion expressed that is in error based on the premise we have a right to life, is the fault of the presenter and not the premise.

On the other hand, any argument presented based on the premise that there are no private property rights would be based on a false premise and, therefore, would be in error every time, without exception. The ACLU is not alone in its attempt to deny our property rights. There are legions that believe government should control all property because individuals are not qualified to manage property to its best use. The managing of property requires the expertise of educated government bureaucrats. Only they have the skill to get the most efficient use of property. My great granduncle practiced selective cutting of his forestland fifty years before it occurred to the Forest Service.

In the Soviet Union, government experts managed agriculture and millions of people starved to death. In Cambodia the results were the same. In North Korea the only chubby person is Kim Jong IL. China is now prospering, but still starvation is common. Do not go to Cuba for lunch unless you like sugar cane. Vietnam is a good place to stay away from. Since we lost the war, there are no reports coming from that nation. One can be sure that things are not well there, just as in South Africa. When the curtain of silence descends over a nation, you can be sure the government is up to mischief against its own people and the rest of the world.

The subject at this moment is offensive aggression. What do all these have to do with offensive violence? Violence is not limited to a roadside bomb going off, or someone punching another in the face. Any act that inhibits one's free use of his property is offensive violence. One should be free to use his property as he pleases just as long as it does not infringe on anyone else's use of their property. It's called the "quiet enjoyment of one's property". Raising pigs in an urban neighborhood would do serious harm to people's quiet enjoyment of their property, and they would not even have to hear the pigs!

I often hear talk-show hosts talk about low-income people who do not pay taxes, especially those who rent and do not own property.

Citizens who live below the poverty line, who pay no income taxes, pay all kinds of taxes -- sales taxes, excise taxes, and real estate taxes (included in the rent they pay). I suppose they could move into a cave. That way they would avoid rent, at least until the owner of the cave came along. With people taking up residence in his cave, he would be arrested for not meeting city codes for rental property. The cave tenants would be okay. It would take months to evict them. If they lived in my community, the owner of the property would have to give them the going rate of two months' rent. The cave dwellers would have to find their own means of moving. The local city council has not thought of the hardship that moving would cause the cave dwellers. I'm sure, as soon as they do, they'll float a bond issue and the problem will be solved for the cave dwellers, but not for those who are going to have to payoff the bond. Sounds silly. This kind of nonsense is really a violation of the property rights of others. In my community, if I buy a vehicle for thirty thousand dollars and the sticker price is thirty-five thousand, I have to pay a sales tax based on the sticker price, not the actual amount I paid. The excise tax is based on the sticker price, not what was actually paid for the vehicle. This is legalized plunder, a violation of my property rights. I am now poorer by the amount that was unjustly taken from me. This act is repeated several times every day, day in and day out. This is another example of the government's creating poverty by committing offensive aggression against me and the citizens of this community.

Social security is the most egregious example of offensive aggression, legalized plunder, and violation of property rights. When Social Security was made into law, retirement age was sixty-five. At that time life expectancy was in the low fifties. Actuarially, no one would live long enough to collect. Today life expectancy is in the seventies with the "baby boomers" about to retire.

Social Security is a Ponzi-type scheme. Charles Ponzi promised to double one's money in ninety days, which he did. The scheme went on well for a while. It depended on a growing group of investors who made it possible for him to pay off those who had invested ninety days earlier. For the most part, those who came in to collect, reinvested their gains. Very little money was paid out.

This is exactly how Social Security works. There has to be enough money coming in from younger workers to pay the benefits of those who have reached retirement age. Not one cent of the younger worker's payment is allowed to be invested in bonds, CD's, or other safe securities.

Charles Ponzi ran out of suckers, and then the roof caved in on him. Shortly Social Security is going to run out of younger workers. One does not want to be standing too close when this one hits the fan.

Defensive Violence

CHAPTER V

U p to this point I have attempted to demonstrate that the number one creator of poverty is government by its violation of Natural Law Property Rights. Denying wholly, or in part, the right to private property creates poverty and, consequently, loss of freedom to the degree that that denial takes place.

By the same token governments can promote prosperity (wealth) by advancing property rights. Under Jack Kennedy a sagging economy was brought back to life by cutting taxes. The cutting of taxes means citizens got to keep more of the fruits of their labor, which in turn promotes commerce. The growth of the economy resulted in greater revenue for the government while at the same time growth in property for the individual. It seems like a contradiction, except it has been proven twice since the presidency of Jack Kennedy.

When Ronald Reagan found himself with a sick economy, he had decided to do what Kennedy had done, cut taxes. Just as happened under Kennedy, Reagan brought the economy back. Government gained more revenue than the amount of the tax cut, and citizens ended up with a gain in wealth.

George Bush did the same thing. If it worked for Kennedy and Reagan, why wouldn't it work for him? Of course, it did. We had record-low unemployment when the Dow hit an all-time high. This happened with ten to twenty million illegal aliens in our midst! But there was mischief afoot. In spite of the warnings of people within the industry, Freddie Mac and Fannie Mae loaned billions upon billions of dollars to individuals who had no way to pay back their loans. Finally, the housing bubble burst.

Failure of the government to perform its duties as determined by Natural Law and the Constitution resulted in the confiscation of private property.

Tax cuts reduce the degree of infringements of private property rights (capitalism), therefore, result in an increase in individual wealth.

It should be recognized that just as government-induced poverty occurs when Natural Law principles are violated, wealth would be produced if those Natural Law violations were corrected. If government limited itself to oversight of the private sector and prevented fraud, theft, price rigging and all of the other sins of the private sector, great prosperity would be the natural consequence. Also, if government did not violate property rights and prevented the private sector from doing so, the degree of wealth and invention would be beyond imagination. The private sector would be driven to discover many secrets of Nature.

The heartbreaking truth of the matter is that the whole world could prosper if this were done everywhere. With food, clothing, and shelter no longer a problem, gifted individuals would give us an explosion of great art, literature, and invention. In America and probably in the world, talented people abound like the grass in the fields. The deserts in the pool of talent could be found in those nations that have no rights to private property. Progress is made in the tools of war in these nations but from knowledge stolen from freer people. *Force without freedom is the antithesis of creativity.*

There are two schools of thought in America. The first and foremost school of thought is that those on the left are convinced that a big government is better. Those on the right prefer a limited government as they see government as a threat to their freedom and to capitalism.

To oppose the unlimited growth of government is an act of defensive aggression mandated by Nature. It cannot be denied that the bigger the government becomes and as more and more power falls into the hands of one person, the poorer that nation becomes. The reference here is not to the United States alone but to all of the nations of the world.

If government were to be limited through democratic means, it would sound extreme to call it defensive aggression. Government is force. Would it be better to call opposition to unlimited government, self-defense? Is the power of the ballot box defensive aggression? If the majority of electors were to believe in enlarging the authority of government, then they would become the means for the state to expand its role of offensive aggression (legalized plunder.). The state can be the source of defensive violence when it acts against criminals who behave in a destructive way. When the state suppresses citizens who are engaged in creative actions, the state becomes the source of destructive aggression. George Washington said, "The price of freedom is eternal vigilance."

That government can expand freedom by protecting property rights is true, but in America it is not very likely. As I sit here and put my thoughts down on an antique computer, my pockets are nearly empty of funds. My competitions are huge government agencies with unlimited funds. To struggle against such huge odds seems foolish, but it is not. After all, what can an individual do against such force? Leonard Read argued, "I should like to counter with the hopeful idea that there is really nothing can be done except by an individual. Only individuals learn. Only individuals can think creatively. Only individuals can cooperate. Only individuals can combat statism."

The soldier protects our property rights and freedom by learning the art of warfare. He is armed. We must stand side by side with our troops armed with an even more powerful weapon.

The knowledge of law given to us by Nature establishes our right to property.

Defensive violence is mandated by Nature. The Creator gave us freewill. Nature does not. The paradox is we are subject to the dictatorship of Natural Law, but we cannot know freedom without subjecting ourselves to her rules. Nature's intent is to promote the survival of the species by driving individuals to struggle with all their strength to survive even to the point where the effort will cause a complete biological breakdown and death.

A person breaks into a home with the intention of burglarizing the dwelling. This is an act of offensive violence. The homeowner confronts the burglar and shoots him, which results in his death. The homeowner has committed an act of defensive violence (self-defense) as mandated by Nature. According to James A. Donald, it is not quite that simple. There has to be a witness to the act to determine who committed offensive aggression and who was defending himself.

He defines the concept of offensive and defensive aggression in his treatise, *Natural Law and Natural Rights*. Person "A" is committing violence against person "B." Person "C", the witness to the act, does not feel threatened by what he sees. Therefore, the action of person "A" is justified. But if the action of person "A" causes person "C", the witness, to feel threatened, then the action of person "A" cannot be justified and constitutes offensive aggression.

Much of the confusion that is encountered is due to the misunderstanding as to what is a "right" and what is a "privilege." We have the right to vote. We have the right to "life, liberty, and the pursuit of happiness". Beyond that, much that is defined as rights, are privileges.

Privileges are favors granted to an individual or group at the expense of someone else. The "right" to a job implies that someone has an obligation to give an individual a job. The "right" to decent housing claims that someone has the obligation to provide housing. The "right" to a living wage demands that the employer pay a living wage, whatever that is? My rights to vote, to the wages I work for, to life, freedom, and the pursuit of happiness do not place an obligation on anyone to furnish those rights to me at their expense.

We can distinguish between a right and a privilege by taking note of who provides it and pays for it. My right to life does not cost anyone anything. Workers pay my Social Security. Therefore, my Social Security is a privilege. There are those who will argue that I paid into Social Security all of my working life; therefore, I have a "right" to my monthly check. This is false. My payments to Social Security went directly toward paying those who met government guidelines. It did not go into an account with my name on it. I did not have the right to withdraw any money from my "account". Every withdrawal from my paycheck that went to the Social Security fund was money that I did not have to spend on my wife, or my children, or myself. If one would take the time to study the Social Security Act, I do not see how anyone could conclude that it is anything, but fraud.

Even if Social Security functioned as advertised, it would be wrong because one is compelled to pay into it under penalty of imprisonment.

Force without freedom is tyranny, and describes every social program managed by government at the city, state and federal level.

It is a direct attack against the private property rights of citizens and a denial of individual freedom. It is the birth of poverty and ultimately evolves into the destruction of the soul.

One can see grass. One can see rain and trees. One can see the force of gravity when one drops something. Nature does not have to be accepted on faith. It can be seen and felt. Nature's Laws are working all around us. It is the heat we feel in our homes and work places in winter. It is the air conditioning in summer. It is the food we eat and the air we breathe. It is the water we drink to quench our thirst, and the water we swim in to enjoy Her embrace. We see Her at Her worst in raging ocean storms, tornadoes, hurricanes, and winter blizzards.

Her laws never need to be updated. There are no loopholes that need to be plugged. Nature does not favor the rich at the expense of the poor.

The violence of Nature is neither offensive, nor defensive -- it is neutral!

It can kill, but it is not its intent to kill. It is without willpower.

It does not even have intelligence!

And yet She is so perfect that Thomas Paine and several of the founders, believed Nature to be God (Deist). It is because of Her perfection that I capitalize Her name every time I use it.

It cannot be stated often enough that citizens should not tolerate any infringements on the right to private property, i.e., earned income. Freedom and one's property are one and the same thing. One cannot stand without the other. The denial of property has reached an alarming level in America. The laypersons feel it in the pits of their stomachs.

They voice their discontent by not voting!

There are many communities in America, run by the government, that are good examples of what a well-managed environment should look like. Shade trees placed perfectly. Acres of lawns as green as the lawn-care commercials. Fences as straight and in as good a condition as the day they were installed. All the buildings in excellent condition. Not a single chip out of the white paint that trims the buildings. The recreation areas are neat and well equipped. The residents are neatly dressed, well fed and get complete medical coverage, free. One might want to visit one of these exemplary communities. They are not difficult to find. There are several in every state. They are called prisons!

When the term "native Americans" is used, it usually refers to whom Columbus erroneously called Indians.

These people should be referred to as *The First Nation,* the *Original People. The rest of us who were born here are native Americans.* We should be referred to as Americans of Irish ancestry, the Americans of African ancestry, etc. We are all Americans. The culture and origins of our ancestors are important; but if we think of ourselves as Americans first, it will contribute to our unity. It might make us all more curious of our American culture that was born in blood and sweat by people who believed that those who would deny the sanctity of private property were criminals who should be killed.

The First Nation was one of the finest cultures on earth. Individual tribes lived in close cooperation with each other -- hunting, gathering and farming. They did not believe that one could own the land, anymore than one could own the rivers, lakes, the ocean, the sky or the sun. They had personal property, but no real estate. They did have wars when one tribe encroached on the other's space. The parents never punished, scolded or screamed at their children. They were brought up by following their parents' example of civil discourse and work, and also by the discipline of warriors.

They had no immunity to the diseases that the Europeans brought here. Measles, small pox and the like just about wiped them out. Unlike the Europeans, they bathed every day regardless of the temperatures.

The Europeans believed any piece of land that did not have a fence around it did not belong to anybody. Needless to say they built fences as quickly as they could. *America has been going downhill ever since.* The First Nation culture was destroyed once the government made them wards of the state. Many of the descendants of proud warriors are now spouse-beating drunks who set miserable examples for their children.

Leonard Read lists five steps that an individual can use to combat statism:

1. Know statism.
2. Become better students of the freedom philosophy and personally practice it at all times.
3. Pass on our findings, orally or in writing, to those who can be interested in them -- especially to those within our own circle of activity.
4. Pass on the ideas or works of others which in our judgement are free of all statist ideas and which have proved helpful to our own thinking. (The approval of any one-statist idea, no matter how minor, is to make the case for the whole caboodle of statism.)
5. Use such educational means as we posses to identify statist ideas as they arise.

One might think that the effort to pass ideas along to others, or even to write an op-ed piece, to be futile. There is no way one can know the influence of the spoken or written word. Forty years ago I rebutted a liberal friend in an op-ed piece that I wrote which appeared in the *Manchester Union Leader* that accused him of practicing "the art of mental gymnastics". Not too long after that op-ed piece appeared I began to see that phrase show up in several publications, and it keeps showing up to this day!

We are not going to change things by having another Boston Tea Party. Although, who knows what changes the recent tea parties might bring about.

To disguise revolutionaries as Indians would be a dead giveaway. Like a literary agent would say, "It's been done." Besides, everybody at the CIA would know because phones are being tapped. Bostonians of today think that patriots are football players. When was the last time that a book was banned in Boston? The disguised Indians would probably be arrested for indecent exposure! Indian costumes cover less of the body than a cheerleader's uniform.

Government has taken a giant step forward in its attack on private property. If one does not avail himself of a voluntary state-sponsored service, one will be fined. The new drug plan works that way. The Massachusetts health plan is hailed as a model for the country. If the uninsured do not buy into the plan, they will be fined a thousand dollars per year. Of course, the probable reason for them to be uninsured is because they do not have a thousand dollars to begin with. Imagine if an auto dealership charged a fine of a couple thousand dollars for not buying their product! That would go far. The auction of the dealership would take place on the first Monday after the sentencing of management.

In Maine, the lobster fishermen must pay the Maine Lobster Promotion Council twenty-five to seventy-five dollars, depending on the class of license they hold, or the state will not issue the fishermen their licenses. An organization that is supposed to work for the benefit of the lobstermen has the power to deny the fishermen their livelihoods if they do not financially support the organization! I do not have to pay the fee because I am over seventy years old, but I cannot have anyone onboard who has not paid the fee. Consequently, the state forces me to fish alone. This puts me in greater danger in what is already the world's most dangerous occupation! I refuse to submit to this form of statism. I refuse to buy lottery tickets because they were first promoted as voluntary taxation.

The council says, "The Maine Lobster Promotion Council is a public instrumentality of the state." It has spent years to disguise itself as some kind of nonprofit or public service agency, when all the time it is a branch of state government. It constantly refers to itself as a nonprofit organization in an attempt to deceive those compelled by law to financially support it.

The similar situation exists with dairy farmers, orange producers, hog farmers, and apple producers. Parallel agencies work to control the harvesting of the ocean, the price of milk and the control of agriculture.

A government cannot control the lobsters, crabs, fish, milk, cows, etc.

A government controls people -- the individual fishermen, farmers, dealers, and processors. It cannot control inanimate objects!

By the use of licenses, the government controls the operators of vehicles, tradesmen and about every activity one can think of.

Perfection

CHAPTER VI

There are those who believe God is perfection. There are those who believe Nature is perfection. Some believe Nature is God or God is Nature. I believe if one obeys the Commandments as I understand them, one would live a holy and productive life. I believe that if one were to obey the Laws of Nature they would live a just and equally productive life. I believe one can live under the rule of God or Nature, one or both, in obedience, and be an exemplary human being.

There are volumes that praise God. There are hymns and music of great beauty that praise the perfection of God. There are fantastic churches from the small colonial-style New England houses of worship to the great cathedrals found around the world.

Nature does not enjoy the devotion that people lavish on God. People do not look at Nature as a means to eternal life. Survival is an extremely strong force that drives humans to heroic efforts to survive even when all odds are against success. If one fails to survive, there is the comfort of faith that one will dwell in the Kingdom of Heaven.

Regardless of the power of one's belief in Natural Law, it cannot promise the blissful existence that a Supreme Being can.

But it is the first precept of Natural Law, self-preservation, which drives the individual to yearn for eternal salvation.

There is biological proof that my dead parents live on through their children, their grandchildren, their great grandchildren and me. My father's sperm fertilized my mother's egg. This resulted in conception and then my birth. His sperm and my mother's fertilized egg live on in me. I pass my sperm on to my children through their mother. This goes on for generation after generation. Even within the Laws of Nature one can have eternal life. It is eternal life without consciousness, which is no life, even if it is biologically correct.

Natural Law is recognized as the basis for a just political system that protects private property rights. Nature holds innumerable secrets that promise a better life each time one of those secrets is discovered.

God is love. Natural Law is science and philosophy. I love and I respect Nature, *so both can dwell in me in perfect harmony.*

There is literature that describes the beauty of Nature. Landscapes fill art museums in oils and watercolors that can take a person's breath away. There is even extensive literature that defines Natural Law. However, the message is not getting through, for some reason. It does seem, though, that the numbers who favor the Constitution and Natural Rights are growing. If this phenomenon is occurring, it is because of the extremes of the left. There is a growing opposition to statism. It is not obvious by the pollsters, but it is certainly obvious as one discusses current events with one's associates -- not scientific to be sure. Future events will be the proof.

Natural Law is a magnificent force with many of its secrets hidden from us. All of the wonders of the world came to us as the secrets of Nature were discovered. There are many thousands of people who seek to discover the secrets of Nature. Also there are many persons who seek to explain Natural Law and Natural Rights. There are many others who deny the existence of Natural Law and Rights.

To study the works of these individuals, one encounters a proliferation of opinions that contradict each other. The confusion occurs as they attempt to define Natural Law as it applies to humans. Other creatures are not mentioned. The mechanical sciences are ignored. The opponents of Natural Law do not recognize that they judge the perfection of Nature by the use of imperfect human minds.

The human mind is corrupt. It has freewill that allows it to say "no" to Nature. All other creatures are superior to humans within the context that they must always say "yes" to Nature. Humans have intrinsic knowledge of right and wrong. Unfortunately, this is not a compass that will guide one through the jungle of imperfect opinions.

Nature is the only guide. Even a corrupt mind must have some common sense. Is there anyone who can logically and rationally deny that each individual has a right to life? With the right to life one has the right to

those things necessary to maintain one's life. Those
things are the fruits of one's labor that constitutes one's
private property. One has the right to exchange one's
property with anyone for property of comparable value as
long as compulsion is not involved. This is what is called
capitalism. Does this sound familiar? It can't be said too
often.

Not one claim can be denied. They are simple and
to the point. No one has the right to take another life
except in self-defense. To take the fruits of another's
labor is to deny him the right to life. To exchange what
belongs to somebody else with another is a crime against
Nature and the life of the true owner. This is "free
enterprise" and a violation of free market and capitalism.
Robbing banks is free enterprise and should not be
confused with a free market or capitalism.

Without Nature, life of any kind could not exist.
There is no way Nature could not exist. It will always
exist just as it has always existed. Is it any wonder that
many believe Nature to be God?

THE RIDDLE OF EPICURUS

Is God willing to prevent evil, but not able?
Then He is not omnipotent
Is He able, but not willing?   Then He is
malevolent.
Is He both able and willing?   Then whence
cometh evil?
Is He neither able nor willing?   Then why call
Him God?

The *Riddle of Epicurus* fails to recognize that
humans have freewill and are subject to the Laws of

Nature. The laws of God and Nature are knowable and compatible. The human species violates these laws at their own peril. It is easier to determine a violation of Natural Law, than a violation of The Commandments. If one holds one's head underwater, the knowledge that Natural Law is being violated will flood into one's brain rather quickly. The punishment is immediate. With the violation of The Commandments, punishment can occur at the time of the infraction or in the future. It depends on how closely the laws parallel each other. Atheists can deny the laws of God, but how can they deny Nature? If they drop a rock on their foot, they would damage it in direct proportion to the size of the rock.

*****

My eighty-year-old sister wishes to sell her house to her daughter. In this community she cannot do this without having the property appraised by the city government. There will be a high appraisal and a low appraisal. The sale price must fall within the high and low appraisal. An attorney must be hired, at my sister's expense, to oversee the sale. Before the deed can be transferred, a second attorney must be hired to guarantee that the first attorney met the provisions of the city codes, again, at my sister's expense.

I have chipmunks, lots of chipmunks, in my yard. They have burrows and dens in great numbers. Not a single chipmunk ever asked me if he could build his dwelling on my property. None ever went to city hall to get permission to build. No Inspectors, plumbing, electrical, construction or occupancy inspectors came to examine their new dwellings. Everything was perfect because they obeyed Nature. They did not have to contend with government mosquitoes. Of course, their ancestors were here long before I was! Therefore, their use of the property predates mine.

Forty years ago my brother laid a large sheet of paper on his kitchen table and subdivided a plot of land into thirty lots. He used a twelve-inch ruler to lay out the streets and the individual lots, including all the dimensions. He took the plan to city hall and that night he had his permits. The cost was one hundred dollars.

It took him three years and six thousand five hundred dollars in fees to build a three-house development, recently. To build a single-family house for his grandson, it cost him six thousand dollars in fees before the foundation was even completed!

*****

Government at all levels needs statistics. Nature does not need any because Nature does not manage our lives nor does it alter its laws. World War II marks the beginning of the decline of property rights. The internment of Americans of Japanese ancestry is the most egregious example. The army rounded them up. We are told over and over again that the army cannot apprehend illegal immigrants from Mexico and that the army cannot be used to seal the border. The sealing of the border is a police matter and not a military duty. Do not tell this to the Iranians or any other ambitious despot.

Government at all levels collects an endless amount of statistics on every activity. It has to have this information in order to manage the lives and businesses of its citizens. As the amount of statistics mounts, freedom diminishes. The individuals have no need for statistics. They are acutely aware of what they have to do to manage their affairs. Nature does not need statistics. Its laws are immutable.

It is easy to find fault with government. Government is so expert at complicating a program until it defies interpretation. The drug program for seniors and the IRS are examples. Natural Law is perfect. One cannot find fault with one's right to life or the right to one's wages to sustain life (private property).

The Search For Nature's Secrets

CHAPTER VII

There are thousands upon thousands of researchers throughout the world who search to discover more of Nature's secrets. Each new discovery improves the quality of life for a few and sometimes that for millions.

The big hunt at the moment is for alternatives to oil. One can be sure that the effort will be successful. The coal miners priced themselves out of the market by their exorbitant demands. Coal as a household energy source was replaced by oil. Oil will be replaced by one of the many alternatives that scientists are feverishly working on at the moment. Arabs will be left to drink their oil or leave it in the ground. Steelworkers did the same thing. Workers who produced structural concrete replaced them. Farmers lost the market for butter to the manufactures of margarine.

Whenever a nation suffers the loss of property to the monopoly of labor in individual industries, entrepreneurs will invent an alternative. Brazil has achieved energy independence. There is no reason why we cannot.

The day is coming when travel from New York to California will be accomplished in the time it will take to think about it. Wars will be fought without troops; cancer will be cured; and a person will die at the age of one hundred. To lose a family member at such a young age will sadden friends and family!

The secrets of gravity will be discovered. If one is in a vehicle that is equipped with a gravity-control device, a tip of a control will cause the machine to move forward or backwards, depending on the wishes of the operator.

Building materials of incredible strength will be developed. Hurricanes and tornadoes will no longer be a problem. Space travel will be as common as traveling on a highway. Ice and windstorms will not cause major power failures because electricity will be transmitted like radio and TV. Crops will be grown inside shelters without the need for soil.

Eighty years ago I was born in a house that did not have electricity or indoor plumbing -- not even central heat! I cannot imagine what wonders of Nature will be discovered in the next eighty years.

Scientists might even discover why the human brain is so numb. America pulled off the greatest economic marvel of all time by governing for one hundred and fifty years under the rule of Nature. Almost everything worth talking about was invented by Americans. For thousands of years farmers plowed their ground with a stick. John Deere came along and invented the steel plow. Now the ground could be plowed deeper and the soil aerated so it could produce more abundant and superior crops. Eli Whitney invented the cotton gin that made it possible for even poor people to wear underwear. (The word "gin" stands for engine.) These two inventions contributed immensely to the American economy. America became an economic world power. If these two inventors knew that they could not profit by their creativity, they would not have produced these tools that increased the productivity per person beyond the imagination of workers. Repeat this burst of productivity by the number of inventions, and one can see one of the reasons why America prospered.

The main reason America prospered was because government operated in harmony with the Laws of "Nature and Nature's God". American citizens are the owners of their creativity, just as I am the owner of the manuscript I am creating. The income for our labor for all of us is our property.

This has been the most successful formula that the world has ever witnessed; and yet the world refuses to follow our lead. Even harder to believe is that great numbers of Americans consider America a failure.

All research is the study of Nature. The private sector spends huge sums on research and development. Government does the same. No scientist searches for new discoveries outside Nature's authority. There is a lot of junk science around which constitutes opinion and not science. True scientific research goes on with little fanfare. Junk science is on the front pages. If one is driving in a long tunnel, there are no left turns or right turns. Natural Law places the same limits on research. To discover anything, one must confine himself to what Nature allows.

The discipline required in search for invention should be the limits we place on our activities. Order is preferred to chaos, especially in one's mind. Creativity is limited to humans, as is freewill. Not being limited by instincts compels people to force themselves to be objective. The subjective part of their thinking has to be kept under control. It is, as one is limited to the use of only part of his brain. Creativity is not limited to those of great intelligence. A child who had tied his shoelaces had performed a creative act. It is a long way from tying one's shoes to building the next generation of super computers; nevertheless, both are creative functions.

As an example, let us use a subject that is familiar to most people -- the Model T Ford. The first one to roll out of the garage door was transportation that was slightly better than a horse and buggy. The big advantage was one did not have to harness the Model T. Crank the motor over by hand, and one of two things could happen. The motor could start, or the crank could kick back and break one's arm. Broken arms are not desirable. The Natural Laws of combustion were applied, and the Model T was equipped with a lever that retarded the ignition spark. This innovation greatly reduced the number of broken arms, but was still not acceptable. After more study of the mechanical Laws of Nature, and viola! -- a major advance into the world of modern wonders, the mechanical starter was invented. No more broken arms! The next step at Ford was to protect the happy owners of Fords from insects. The bugs in their teeth betrayed the happy owners! The next great step in the evolution of the automobile was the development of the windshield. These were made of plain glass. One did not have to hit a tree very hard for the passenger's head to go through the glass. This is how the passenger side of a vehicle became known as the suicide corner. The steering wheel stopped the driver from hitting the windshield; however, headless passengers were not a good testimonial for Ford. That was a bad thing!

Along with the great improvements in interior comfort, the scientists who studied the quirks of Nature developed safety glass, and at about that time took a giant step into the world of materialism by developing an in-car radio. The radios worked best if one drove on the opposite side of the road away from the power lines. This was not the safest thing to do because the vehicle was constantly crossing over into the oncoming lane.

Oh, the wonders of science and Nature. With the nice seats and radio, it was time to put heat in what had become a closed-in vehicle. It was at this point that researches forgot the Laws of Nature. They built a sheet-metal device that wrapped around the exhaust manifold that directed the exhaust heat into the passenger compartment. Unfortunately, it also directed exhaust fumes into the passenger compartment, killing the passengers.

"Back to the drawing board," as the saying goes. The hot water heater was born. This went a long way in keeping a company's customer base in tact. It is enough to drive one foolish. Solve one problem, and here comes another. Comfortable heat, equals high humidity, equals fogged-up windows, equals more accidents. This time the car owners solved the problem by the installation of fans that blew air on the windshield and helped to keep it clear. It wasn't the best setup, but it was much better than nothing.

There was another problem with visibility. Windshield wipers operated by vacuum motors.

The more one pushed down on the gas pedal, the slower the wipers worked. On a steep grade, they stopped. Nature could not win all of the battles. The engineers did away with vacuum motors and replaced them with electric. Another problem solved.

This single product, the automobile, has brought about research that has greatly improved the product, the quality of life of the consumer and a huge boost to the economy. The most important contribution has been that each improvement has expanded our knowledge of Natural Law.

The development of computers and computer software has had an equal impact. The development of satellite technology has contributed significantly to our acquisition of knowledge. Every bit came about through the discovery of more of Nature's secrets.

Nature drives the individual to survive, reproduce and acquire knowledge. The drive to survive is what brings about the endless search to develop products and services that improve our quality of life. The products of industry are constantly upgraded. It is best if there is a teenager in the household to teach those of us who are not so young anymore how to operate the electronic wonders that seem to come about every day.

One never knows where government is going next. Because the IRS rules one way today, it does not follow that it will rule the same way tomorrow. Government is as predictable as the stock market, which is to say, totally unpredictable. Nature can be relied upon to be consistent. Ocean tides can be predicted for the next umpteen years with perfect accuracy. The rise and fall of the tides can be forecast to the inch, twice a day for years in advance. Sunrise and sunset is known in advance to the minute and the phases of the moon. The next eclipse is known years in advance. There is nothing humans can do to alter these facts. There is nothing that humans can do to alter Nature. She is the core to every action in the universe from a person eating a hotdog to the fusion of the sun. It is said that necessity is the mother of invention. This is not true. Knowledge of Nature is the mother of invention.

Many years ago, as a lobster fisherman, I tried to develop a lobster trap that would outfish anything in use at the time. Not only is lobstering a dangerous occupation; the competition among lobstermen is ferocious and sometimes violent.

I built a trap, often called a lobster pot, made of Sears Roebuck galvanized welded fence wire. It caught twice the lobsters of a wooden trap. The cost of the trap was three times that of a wooden trap. I was able to keep the secret from my competitors for two years or better. Today wire traps are exclusively used. Since then, I've come up with other little "inventions" to give me a slight edge. We watch each other like hawks. As one-man makes an improvement, others soon will follow. We know Nature. We just about live in her lap. If we find ourselves in conflict with Nature, we resolve the problem as quickly as possible. It takes a dry boat to float. If suddenly flooding is detected, all activity stops with the exception of determining the source of the flooding. If it is not found quickly, other vessels nearby are requested to keep an eye on us until the problem is resolved. It is this buddy system that prevents mortality from getting completely out of hand.

There are those who will charge that the views expressed are an oversimplification. Those who make such a charge will be the ones who overcomplicate a subject. Of what good is it to the layperson if a discussion goes into such depth as to be beyond the comprehension of but a few? Einstein was completely understood by one or two others in the world. The rest did not have to understand in order to enjoy the benefits of his theories.

Others were brilliant enough to explain his discoveries so that great numbers were able to grasp the concept.

It is not necessary that citizens have a philosopher's comprehension of private property in order to defend their right to property. People know that their wages belong to them and nobody else. They know that the things they purchase with their wages belong to them and are their property. What they do not know is how to recognize demagoguery. Too many consider themselves to be in the middle, politically. They are proud to be independents. They vote the candidate, and not the party. They are neither on the right, nor on the left. Actually, they are nowhere. They are not Democrats or Republicans. What they do not realize is that they arrive at their political position because of their lack of knowledge of Natural Law. Hopefully, someday they will be able to recognize their Natural right to property as easily as they can recognize that the money on their person is their property.

Economics

CHAPTER VIII

"Capitalism is the guaranteed uneven distribution of wealth.
"Socialism is the guaranteed even distribution of poverty." (Jason Lewis)

Freedom economics is the complex evolution of the hunting and gathering culture of human origin based on Natural Law private property rights. (The Author)

Contemporary industrial economics "is the social science that studies the production and consumption of goods and services." (Wikipedia)

Our original ancestors depended completely on what Nature provided. It is the same today, but people do not deal directly with Nature in the raw; they deal with the supermarkets. Their dependency on Nature is not as obvious as it was to the hunters and gatherers of antiquity.

If one of the original people was accosted and had the success of his hunt taken from him, he knew that his property had been taken. Today everything from your identity to your property, are easy targets for the unscrupulous.

Payroll deductions are the greatest idea that government ever had to separate individuals from their earnings (private property) and keep the protest down to a minimum. I can see politicians enjoying the movie *Popeye* and saying, "Why can't we do that -- the baby-crying tax, the crossing-the-street tax?"

The laws of economics are truly within the domain of Natural Law. It is here that Nature is violated in every way that warped minds can conceive. It is they who promote poverty of the mind and body.

Poverty is a violation of Natural Law! Eliminate Natural Law Private Property Rights violations, and poverty would disappear.

Humans possess intelligence and cunningness. It is debatable which of the two dominates human activity. Intelligence is the ability of the mind to think, reason and learn. Cunningness is shrewdness, craftiness, and skill in deception and guile. Greed dominates the cunning individual. Greed is good when prevented from acting in a destructive way. If government would prevent the destructive use of greed, the greedy person or persons would be forced to satisfy their greed while engaged in creative activity. They can only satisfy themselves by supplying the public with goods and services. I suspect that the greedy create wealth to a greater degree than the benevolent entrepreneurs.

When one considers that the individual mind is a combination of greed and intelligence, then this amounts to splitting hairs. The state should do its duty and prevent destructive actions from taking place against its citizens. In an orderly society where Nature rules, regardless of the population of the community, there will be numerous merchants all acting independently one from the other. Yet there will be everything that people will need with a minimum of waste. The invisible hand in action!

Put a government committee in charge of procuring for the community, and there will be shortages of some goods. Waste will be rampant. The biggest shortage will be money allocated for the community budget.

Natural Law is freedom and private property that translates to the right to life. If scams were crude oil, America would be energy independent. It is amazing that the private sector survives with the siege being directed at it. Every homeowner is part of the private sector. The operator of the hotdog wagon is also part of the private sector.

Every dollar one spends outside the public sector contributes to the success of the private sector. Each dollar spent is a vote for the longevity of the company that produced the product purchased. If the product does not satisfy the consumer, he can immediately withdraw his support without having to wait four years before the opportunity to vote again.

In the minds of the private property abolitionists, the foulest word in any language is profit. To him or her, for anyone to make a profit, means that they engaged in price gouging. If they had their way, the penalty for making a profit would be greater than the penalty for cheating "widows and orphans". They would have all of their property confiscated for distribution, in equal shares, to the various government agencies. With the extra money, they could create jobs in their agency. With the increase of employees, instead of three months to get a reply to a request, it would take three and a half months. A private sector company could perform the same task in minutes by e-mail, or three weeks by government snail mail.

Profit is the engine that drives capitalism. It is the bottom line when one exchanges his property for someone else's. Both parties believe that the exchange resulted in a profit for each of them. A person exchanges his property because he values the property of another more than he values his own.

Consumers hate the high price of fuel, but they have to have it. They pay the price because they need the fuel more than the money it costs, not to mention the loss in wages if they do not get to work.

Without the profit that wages represent, why would one bother to get out of bed in the morning?

There are endless new products and services provided at the entrepreneur's risk every year. If the venture fails, a serious loss of money occurs. If it is successful, like with Bill Gates, then the anti-capitalist mental midgets will use every bit of legal skullduggery to destroy the individual or his enterprise, preferably both.

Profit is a roof that protects the consumer. An enterprise must operate efficiently and give good service along with good products or it will fail. Put this together with a government that protects private property, and one has a formula for prosperity.

Government does not have to make a profit. There is no roof to limit the amount of funds it squanders. It does not have to be efficient, provide reasonable service, or even be pleasant. Government's tax base grows by leaps and bounds, particularly on the local level. This allows for constantly growing revenues, and yet local taxes go up every year.

In the city of Laconia, NH, a candidate for mayor argued that if he were elected he would bring about the purchase of the privately owned water works. He convinced the voters that with city ownership, there would be no need to make a profit; therefore, the voters would save money on their water bills.

Customers of the Water Company paid their water bills once a year. Within a few months of city's ownership, the city billed its customers twice a year. The bill was the same amount semi-annually that the private company charged annually!

When the Water Company was privately owned, it maintained the water mains and lines going into homes. With new construction, they installed lines from the water main to the foundation. It was the owner's responsibility to extend the line through the foundation.

By the end of the first year of municipal ownership, it was the consumers' responsibility to construct and maintain the lines from the water main into their buildings. Within a few years, the cost of water went up four hundred percent! That was quite a difference from private ownership. Lakes surround Laconia, NH. It has enough fresh water to supply the needs of Boston and New York several times.

The anti-property crowd constantly belittles capitalism. The socialists or near-socialist nations have no way of pricing goods and services. They have to study prices in capitalist nations to determine what to charge for goods and services. Prices are set by the state. Food markets are fully inventoried with empty shelves. It is a mystery that I have never been able to solve. It is the intelligencia who promotes the denial of property rights. Where they succeed in bringing about a totalitarian state, they are the first ones who are put up against the wall and shot. This was true in Communist Russia, China, North Korea, Cuba, Vietnam and, the worst of all, Cambodia's Khmer Rouge, who were responsible for the deaths of one point seven million to three million citizens.

I can read, write, and speak in French. This was the language of Cambodia. I had the opportunity to speak, at length, to a Cambodian who survived Pol Pot. His description of the march from the cities into the countryside to establish an agrarian culture was bone chilling. His description of life once they were settled was even worse. There was no food. A rat was a feast. They ate grass and the bark from trees. The beatings alone were enough to cause one to pray for death!

When economic freedom does not exist in a nation, that nation has reached the depth of corruption. The human mind is as ingenious in being destructive as the creative mind is in being constructive.

Let us look at inflation. In almost every publication where an article appears on the subject of inflation, the blame will be put on the worker who demands higher wages. This is a reasonable conclusion when one considers that the price of everything is the cost of labor that produces it. If I'm a carpenter and I have work done by a plumber, he in turn employs me to do carpentry work for him. Ours are comparable skills that the market values the same. What difference does it make if we charge each other fifty cents an hour or fifty dollars an hour?

Everything is fine as long as the monetary system is not tampered with. As an extreme example, we will say that government doubles the amount of money in circulation. This will not affect our friends, the carpenter and plumber, as far as the value of the work they did for each other. It is when they go out to purchase the goods and services of others. Now they find out that their money is worth half as much as it was before the government inflated the money supply.

If we take the total value of the nation's goods and services, and then total the amount of cash in circulation, the value of all our goods and services can be determined in dollar amounts. Now, if the treasury doubles the amount of cash in circulation, the prices of everything will double. Not one cent in wealth would have been gained. If one wishes to look up inflation in an unabridged Webster dictionary, one will find basically the same definition I have made.

I grew up during the great depression. We were as poor as poor could get. People who lived in fishing villages were considered as coming from the wrong side of the tracks. If it had not been that we lived on the ocean, we probably would have starved. It seemed odd that such a poor family survived on clams, lobster, cod and haddock. Once in awhile we would have meat loaf. Sometimes on Sunday, we would have chicken fricassee. The chicken was an old hen that no longer laid eggs. It was tougher than an oak log. Mixed in a white gravy and cut up into small, less than bite size pieces, it made a great feast for a large, depression time family.

America the wonderful -- my seven brothers and sisters all became wealthy.

They achieved their success at a time when America was a nation of laws. No more, we now have a government of outlaws.

Observe the gray squirrel. It is constantly searching for food. It is alert to all of the dangers that could threaten its life. In the cities it moves about more at ease. There are no hawks or foxes to pounce on it. It knows that humans will not harm it. In the country it is shy. There are too many predators. It never strays into open spaces, but makes sure that there is an escape nearby such as trees or brush. If one is careful to earn its trust, it will eat out of one's hand; but if that trust cannot be established, the squirrel will not go near humans.

The squirrel has a pure mind. The DeVinci Code is of no concern to it. It is ruled by Nature, and its daily actions are driven by its instincts. Its economics is limited to finding enough food for it to survive.

With humans, food, clothing, and shelter have to be manufactured. This requires innumerable interchanges with endless numbers of people. (Read Leonard Read's, *"I Pencil".)* Industries move to where they can get skilled labor at the lowest price. They have to have raw materials. They have to hire economists to keep them on the right track. Corporations, big and small, have to be competitive in price and quality. The private sector is complicated, difficult, stressful and constantly under attack by the anti-property crowd. As an individual, all one needs to know is a simple formula that will make it possible to distinguish right actions by business and government -- MMW=NR+HEXT -- *man's material welfare is equal to natural resources plus human effort times tools.*

Natural resources and human effort are limited. There is no limit on tools. A great story about tools is the story of R. G. Letourneau. He went into the construction business several times. Every time he went bankrupt. In the process of fulfilling his construction contracts, Letourneau would modify the equipment of the day to make it more efficient than the equipment of his competitors. At the bankruptcy auctions, other contractors bid high enough for Letourneau's improved construction tools that he actually turned a profit. Finally, he quit as a contractor and became very successful as a manufacturer of construction equipment.

Robots, for instance, can produce twenty-four hours a day, never having to stop to eat or sleep and can produce endless products with a minimum of human supervision.

All laws that fall within the limits of this formula will promote wealth. All rules that violate the formula are a violation of the Natural Laws of Economics and, consequently damage the economy and contribute, to a degree, to poverty.

Economic damage is done in a democratic society because elections are beauty contests. The candidates can know little, or nothing, of what is being discussed here. They hire speechwriters who are clever enough to convince the voter that up is down, rich is bad, and that SUV's are going to be the death of all of us. They also can convince the voter that each tree that is cut down will increase global warming by 10%; and if they vote for the opposition candidate, the world will come to an end!

Is it too much to ask that candidates at least know what the founders meant when they included in the Declaration of Independence, "The Laws of Nature and Nature's God"? They should understand the difference between primary knowledge and secondary knowledge. They should know that America is the mother of invention. Do any of them know why America prospered beyond anything that ever existed on earth? Do they ever wonder when other nations steal our science, the Americans come back in a heartbeat, and make the stolen technology obsolete?

They should know what capitalism is and how it works.

And shouldn't we know why the largest assembly of the super rich, who make up our Congress, are constantly condemning the rich? Is it shadow boxing? Do they pay their taxes? There are so many there who pervert their Nature for personal gains that it has become pretty much their national pastime. As the government grows more corrupt, so then does the nation.

America is the refuge for those forced into poverty by their governments. We are beginning to follow in the footsteps of foreign states.

*****

From the Foundation of Economic Education --

Clichés of Socialism NUMBER 7:

"Why, you'd take us back to the horse and buggy."

The basic fallacy of this all too-common cliché is confusion between technology and such other aspects of human life as morality and political principles. Over the centuries, technology tends to progress; from the first wheel to the horse and buggy to the railroad and the jet plane. Looking back on this dramatic and undeniable progress, it is easy for men to make the mistake of believing that all other aspects of society are somehow bound up with, and determined by, the state of technology in each historical era. Every advance in technology, then, seemingly requires some sort of change in all other values and institutions of man. The Constitution of the United States was, undoubtedly, framed during the "horse and buggy" era. Doesn't this mean that the railroad age required some radical change in that Constitution, and that the jet age requires something else? As we look back over our history, we find that since 1776, our technology has been progressing, and that the role of government in the economy, and in all of society, has also grown rapidly. This cliché simply assumes that the advance of technology must have required the growth of government.

If we reflect upon this idea, the flaws and errors stand out. Why should an increase in technology require a change in the Constitution, or in our morality or values? What moral or political change does the entrance of a jet force us to adopt?

There is no necessity whatever for morality or political philosophy to change every time technology improves. The fundamental relations of men, their need to mix their labor with resources in order to produce consumer goods, their desire for sociability, their need for private property, to mention but a few are always the same, whatever the era of history. Jesus' teachings were not applicable just to the ox-cart age of first-century Palestine; neither were the Ten Commandments somehow "out-moded" by the invention of the pulley.

Technology may progress over the centuries, but the morality of man's actions is not thereby assured; in fact, it may easily and rapidly retrogress. It does not take centuries for men to learn to plunder and kill one another, or to reach out for coercive power over their fellows. There are always men willing to do so. Technologically, history is indeed a record of progress; but morally, it is an up-and-down and eternal struggle between morality and immorality, between liberty and coercion.

While no specific technical tool can in any way determine moral principles, the truth is the other way round: in order for even technology to advance, man needs at least a modicum of freedom. Freedom to experiment, to seek the truth, to discover and develop the creative ideas of the individual. And remember every new idea must originate in some one individual.

Freedom is needed for technological advance; and when freedom is lost, technology itself decays and society sinks back, as in the Dark Ages, into virtual barbarism.

The glib cliché tries to link liberty and limited government with the horse and buggy; socialism and the welfare state, it slyly implies are tailored to the requirements of the jet and the TV set. But on the contrary, it is socialism and state planning that is many centuries old, from the savage Oriental despotisms of the ancient empires to the totalitarian regime of the Incas. Liberty and morality had to win their way slowly over many centuries, until finally expanding liberty made possible the great technological advance of the Industrial Revolution and the flowering of modern capitalism. The reversion in this century to ever-greater statism threatens to plunge us back to the barbarism of the ancient past.

Statists always refer to themselves as "progressives," and to libertarians as "reactionaries." These labels grow out of the very cliché we have been examining here. This "technological determinist" argument for statism began with Karl Marx and was continued by Thorstein Veblen and their numerous followers – the real reactionaries of our time. (MURRY N. ROTHBARD)

It Is the Nature of Things

CHAPTER IX

If one falls out of a boat into the water, one will get wet, of that there is no doubt. The nature of water is liquid. If one is having a cookout on a beach and steps on the hot coals in their bare feet, one will get burnt. That is the nature of fire. The nature of government is to fend off, to stop. That is why the enforcers of government rules carry guns. You will pay your Social Security, or you will be killed. If the police use force to arrest you for not complying, and you resist with your own force, sooner or later you'll end up dead. To surrender is to comply. This might sound like a stretch, but as the stunt man warns, "Don't try this at home."

Government is organized force. Organized force without freedom is tyranny. Organized force that defends freedom is justice. Eliminate freedom, and what is left is force. Freedom dies a little at a time. I have lived eighty plus years. I was born in one of the nicest houses in our neighborhood in 1926. Along came the big depression and the bank ended up with our home. My family moved into a house that was owned by my grandmother. It was without electricity or indoor plumbing. It was intended for summer occupancy. The one good thing about it -- we did not have to worry about the plumbing freezing. The interior was unfinished. The framing was visible because there were no inside walls. When the wind blew, which was all of the time, it came through the house with sufficient velocity to blow the blankets off the beds. Well, maybe it was not quite that bad; but when Papa lit his pipe, he had to be sure that he had his back to the windward side of the building.

The big deal, the really big deal -- we were free! Papa made his home brew. Everybody told him he made the best home brew anywhere. As tough as things were, that home brew was the reason for some great parties and leaps of joy. We little ones had a great time as we peeked down the stairs and watched the grown-ups square dance. There was no welfare back then. The busybody government had not been invented. The Constitution was the law of the land.

We dug clams to get by, and ate a lot of them as well as sold some on the side of the road. We did not have a vendor's license or a health department certification. We did not have a stainless steel table or state-approved containers with bar codes and nutritional information. We were left alone. We were free to get by on our own ingenuity. I worked on a farm for twenty-five cents an hour. There was no minimum wage. Everybody, who was willing to work, found work. Even in those times, my father told us many times over that there was always work to be found, but much of it was work that many refused to do. Men, women, and children suffered in those days, but it is those hard times that produced the world's greatest generation -- the persons who won World War II.

It was those hard times and World War II that gave birth to busybody government and an end to strict adherence to Natural Law Private Property Rights. Unfortunately this came about because people wanted it. They preferred security to freedom. At the rate we are now going, one day we will have neither. We have digressed to the point where Congress is having a spirited debate as to whether English is going to be the official language in America! It is the international language of commerce, but fools do not think it should be our official language? What is next? Shall we do away with the eagle and the rest of our national symbols? For fifty years the same fools have said that God is dead. They would say the same of Nature, but they think that Nature is global warming, a sandy beach, and sex. How do the environmentalists explain the fact that the temperature on Mars is way below freezing and yet its atmosphere is totally carbon dioxide?

.

*****

Where did all of the oil come from that is everywhere under the surface of planet earth? There must have been some serious global warming a million or more years ago. The oil formations did not occur during the ice ages. Then there is the problem of our moon gradually moving away from us. Eventually it will no longer cause the tides, the wobble in earth's rotation or the consequent control of our seasons. Arctic weather could ultimately occur anywhere on the planet, even in the tropics! The most alarming threats to earth are asteroids. One solid hit could eliminate all life.

Sooner or later one of these events will occur. It will probably be an asteroid strike. Our planet is doomed.

It is inevitable. It will probably happen when our sun cools down. Such an event is so far off into the future that it is ridiculous to concern us now.

The greatest threat to humankind comes from humans. That is what should concern everyone. It is imperative for the majority to become literate and able to distinguish slight violations of Natural Law Private Property Rights from out-and-out legalized plunder.

Presently the economy is booming. (At this writing the crash had not occurred.) The Dow is about to break its all-time record. Unemployment is under five percent, which equals full employment. The constant barrage of gloom and doom has convinced the general public that we are in bad times. The ever increase in the efficiency of tools and tax cuts prove otherwise. With more money in their pockets, consumers have more to spend or invest. Capitalism is doing fine in spite of the barrage of interference that comes from Washington and the environmentalists. This proves the strength of the free market that we can prosper even when shackled to a welfare state. Until everyone has everything they desire, there will be no shortage of work. Poverty is not due to the lack of work available but by the short-circuiting of the Natural Laws of economics.

*****

Socialism is the most perfect economic system devised by humans. "From each according to his means; to each according to his needs." In theory, Socialism is like water going over a dam. Each drop is identical to every other drop. It is without intelligence, instincts or knowledge, and yet, as it passes through the turbine, it produces power. Power that can be used to build machines, drive appliances, and light the world.

The advocates of the perfection of Socialism forget the imperfections of those who are going to be forced to practice it. Capitalism is infused into the Nature of humans. Socialism wages war on human Nature.

"To each according to his means. To each according to his needs," results in workers who have no incentive to work. With Capitalism, what I grow on my acre of land is mine. The more work I put into it, weeding and fertilizing, the greater the productivity and the greater the profit. With millions of workers driven by the profit motive and the belief that what they earn is theirs, the more powerful the economy will be. With Capitalism, workers strive to produce more. With Socialism, workers do as little as they can. This is the Nature of humans. It cannot be changed, even at the point of a gun, just as water cannot be forced to flow uphill.

One does not have to live in a socialist society to suffer the effects of political intervention. Socialism is one hundred percent intervention. Capitalism is political intervention to the degree needed to prevent the private sector from acting destructively such as false advertising, the creation of monopolies, the production of shoddy goods, the use of force, etc.

The more intrusive government becomes, the less productivity an enterprise will experience. This is particularly true with the self-employed and small employers. The paperwork involved -- reports that one must read, fill out, return -- and the regulation that one must obey, takes time that could be better spent in production. The fishing industries, like all enterprises, are particularly being damaged under mounds of red tape. Freedoms no longer exist on the high seas. There are government tracking devices on fishing vessels that show where the vessels are at all times. There is also a live government observer. There are severe restrictions as to the number of days that one can fish and where. Nature does not take its toll only on the fishermen. Vessels that cost in the millions sit idle, rusting away. Commercial vessels have to be in constant use or they deteriorate faster than when they were in use.

*****

The nature of government force is such that the fewer individuals who share power with a head of state, the greater the poverty in such nations. When all power is in the hands of one individual, poverty is complete.

Nature cannot be changed. The creatures of the world are spectators that live at the mercy of Nature. If She does not give us rain, we all go hungry. If She strikes us with destructive storms, all must run for shelter. Humans can direct all of their energy to alter Nature, but the effort will be as futile as a squirrel that tries to stand in the middle of a highway to stop a trailer truck. The puny efforts of humans to stop global warming are even better examples.

Humans are a different story. They are fickle. They can be affected by everything from a master debater to superstition. The public school system is designed to dumb down children. Geography, history, science, and math are nearly unknown to them. In nineteen hundred, to pass from grade school to high school, students had to pass exams that college graduates could not pass today.

It seems as if humans have intrinsic knowledge. No matter how exposed they are to untruths, people feel that something is not right. The American Republic has survived longer than any other in history, in spite of endless misinformation. For the past sixty-five years, our nation has survived, wounded, but not critically, yet. How did the great minds of history discover the secrets of Nature? (Thomas Paine, Adam Smith, John Locke, and the founders of our Republic?)

It must be a yearning for freedom that burns in the human soul. The French Revolution was driven by a yearning for freedom. (By the way, the only war that the French have ever won was the French Revolution and that was because it was Frenchmen fighting Frenchmen!) The American Revolution was a fight for freedom. It was an effort to get out from under the English heel to escape "taxation without representation".

When there were a few humans, they were free. Do the remnants of that brand of freedom linger still in our minds and souls? Will it be able to withstand the forces of evil that pervades our nation? Considering the origin of freedom in the human mind, the nature of the human mind has to be liberty. The yearning for freedom is not one of the three natural inclinations of humans, but is a condition of the human animal as it moves through life. The confusion of rational thought has to be the fault of freewill, the ability to choose Nature or evil. No other creature has that ability; therefore, no other creature is free to violate its Nature. They are limited to act in accordance to their instincts.

The Nature of poverty is caused by the evil actions of others. There are thieves, swindlers, and governments. The chief cause of poverty is government action. A woman with three children is on welfare. Every time she spends some of her welfare money, there are several taxes on every dollar. This is insane. She gets state assistance, then the state taxes her welfare check! With reform of the welfare system, she now has to go to work. So who takes care of her three children? Talk about being between a rock and a hard place.

If the state had not stepped out of its role of being the protector of Natural Law Private Property Rights and stayed out of the social life of its citizens, there would be few single-parent homes. If men can relieve themselves of the responsibility of financing their families by having babies out of wedlock, then there are going to be many single-parent homes. *That is the Nature of the beast.*

Power

CHAPTER X

Power is the hell that all humans have to live with. Many citizens are controlled completely by their rulers. The degree of control varies from one nation to the next. In America we like to believe we enjoy a degree of freedom greater than anywhere else. The question of the power that one is subjected to is strictly a human problem. All other creatures are free, for the most part, of being dominated by a single powerful leader. Within a family of wolves there exists the alpha male. The alpha male is a reality of some other creatures. Alpha-male dominance is limited to the members of its extended family, not its entire species.

The history of humanity has been of one psychopath after another who trics to enslave the population of the planet. None has ever succeeded, but this does not stop the drive of some to go where others failed. The human mind is corrupt and corrupted. Freewill gives it the option to obey or disobey Nature. A constant barrage of misinformation makes it difficult to determine right from wrong. In the beginning, humans were no different than the extended families of other animals. They were hunters and gatherers. They had few possessions and the food they found they consumed as they continued to look for other sources of nourishment. Almost all of their waking hours were used to feed themselves. If one observes chipmunks, squirrels, the birds of the sky, and the fish of the ocean, one will see behavior identical to that of our original ancestors.

Natural inventiveness and curiosity of the corrupt human mind discovered the benefits of agriculture. Soon a combination of hunting and farming became the culture of our earliest ancestors. Humans prospered. The discovery and development of agriculture evolved into commerce, which brought into existence the cesspools of human kind -- cities!

Without agriculture and cities, the population of humans would have been controlled in the same way as the population of all other creatures. When food is abundant, populations grow. The greater population brings about shortages. Shortages cause a decrease in population, and the cycle goes on over and over.

As the combination of hunting and gathering progressed, family groups mixed. Now the need for rules of behavior became necessary. A ruler was selected and *political power over others was born. This was the birth of government.*

First there was the family. Families gave rise to government; therefore, all government authority arises from its citizens. The state cannot have any rights not first held by its citizens. The family is the basic unit of government. To destroy the authority of Nature and the family, the family has to be destroyed as the basic unit of society. Americans of African ancestry had strong family units. After a slave owner completed the sale of one of his slaves, the slave's family was without a husband and a father. The slave took an ax and cut off one of his hands. He was then worthless to the prospective buyer and was punished severely. To the slave it was worth his sacrifice to keep his family together.

Strong families continued after slavery and all of the abuse that former slaves were put through. Strong ties to their churches held the community together. It was not until the beginning of the welfare state that Black culture began to be damaged. In the meantime, the white community was under attack by the ACLU, environmentalists, and other anti-capitalists who have successfully cast the Christians as a fringe group out of the mainstream of American culture.

Both Black and White families are falling apart. Children are no longer disciplined in school. Should parents strike out-of-control children in their own homes, they will be prosecuted. Over and over we hear that it is the parents' fault that children are out of control. Parents and teachers are without power. Of course, children will take advantage of the situation. Each day the family unit becomes weaker. Each day government grows bigger and stronger.

It is said that "power corrupts and absolute power corrupts absolutely". The American government's power is out of control and is going to have to be curbed before it becomes totally out of control. It would not be surprising, in the event of another 9/11, to see martial law declared. That would be the end of our freedom.

The power of a great nation is being challenged by a group of savages who know no boundaries to their viciousness. They wage war against the finest troops that ever existed in the history of the world. They have power. They use it against our troops and our allies. They strike at the holy places of their fellow Muslims. They kill their brothers in the market places. They attack women. They kill children while they study in the schools that had been refurbished by the American soldier who they are too cowardly to fight face to face.

When one of their suicide bombers carries out his mission, the remains of the bomber should be gathered and buried with a pig or a dog. I wonder how many of them would want to spend eternity in hell with a pig as a companion, instead of going to heaven with a busload of his very own virgins?

The mobs that ravage France and the gangs in the US have the same kind of power as the suicide bomber. They use it the same way -- against unarmed civilians with no way to protect themselves. These are the twenty-first-century "warriors". What miserable excuses for manhood? If any of them want to see a real warrior, let them look at an American soldier eye to eye. That GI represents the finest in defensive violence (self-defense). The insurgency represents the worst in offensive violence, as it is in clear violation of Natural Law.

Power does not always come from the barrel of a gun. It can come from the end of one's arms in the form of a fist. When confronted by a gun or a fist, the power that they represent is immediately obvious to an individual. The power of the media is subtle. (Hitler argued that a lie that was told often enough becomes believable.) It has great influence on the direction that a nation takes. It can make or destroy reputations at will. The citizens of Maine had the option to vote a tax cap, similar to California's Proposition 13. Maine citizens are the most heavily taxed in the country. The state's newspapers began a campaign to convince the voters that the tax cap would be catastrophic for the communities.

There would be a loss of teachers, police, and firefighters. It would result in the loss of millions upon millions of federal-matching funds. These arguments were all fallacious. To the total surprise of the supporters of the tax cap, the proposition was defeated. People constantly complain about high taxes. Every bond issue passes after the local media spends a year before the vote to convince all that the bonds are great ideas.

The political right always complains about the power of the New York Times. Actually, the small-town newspapers have a greater influence than the Times. For the most part, they parrot the Times. People who have never held a copy of the Times are reading stories that were first printed in the Times.

*****

The greatest power of all is knowledge. One can not put together a great enterprise without knowledge. It takes great skill to successfully manage a company and keep it a step ahead of its competition. The power of the ballot box cannot be used effectively without the knowledge of Natural Law Private Property Rights. Voting power is the only way that the trend toward statism can be reversed.

In researching political power one finds oneself in a quagmire of philosophies that can be enlightening, but seem more like conflicting opinions by the thousands. It is essential for the benefit of scholars. It is not necessary for the average layperson. One is interested to know enough to be able to protect his property and freedom from ambitious and mischievous government agencies. By understanding our rights under the authority of Nature, which takes precedence over the Constitution, one's power precedes the power of the state. In no way can individual power alter the power of Nature. It can alter the power of government. The American Revolution is a case in point. *Natural Law existed millions of years before governments.* Therefore, any law devised by humans that attempts to alter Natural Law is an unjust law. (Martin Luther King, Jr.) The sponsors and supporters of such laws should be voted out of office.

Nature had no beginning, nor will it ever end. It is incapable of error because it does not possess willpower or intelligence. It cannot show mercy in a storm or benevolence that causes crops to grow. It is the ultimate in power. Even the mighty US Air Force scatters out of the path of a major storm. Those who think puny humans can alter Nature are laboring under a false premise. If humans create conditions that one conceives as damaging to Nature, it is Nature that will eliminate humans.

The most powerful thing possessed by people is an idea. The American idea is -- *all are created equal and have the right to* "*life, liberty, and the pursuit of happiness*" *given to them under the* **authority** *of the* "*Laws of Nature and Nature's God.*" No law devised by mankind can overrule this authority.

The American colonists challenged the most powerful government on earth. Poorly armed and trained, they defeated the English superpower. It was the American idea of freedom that drew the guns that were sufficient to drive the English off the American soil.

The idea that Christ preached to all who would listen has been understood in different ways. There has been endless strife and wars of one group after another as they try to impose their _opinions_ of the teachings of Jesus.

The present war by radical Muslims against "infidels" is the latest example.

Nations will suffer under the power of unjust rulers, generation after generation, without rebelling. However, once their superstitions are challenged, they will go to their deaths to defend them.

Beginning in 1692, the Salem witch-hunt was an instance where members of a community condemned their neighbors of witchcraft. This was an example of superstition that was limited to a community. Catholicism in South America is an example of people who belonged to a legitimate church and modified half of its liturgy into acts of superstition. The worship of Mary is an example.

It becomes obvious that power has many forms and when misused, people suffer. Socialism (Communism) has been the cause of sixty to a hundred million deaths worldwide. Other totalitarian governments have murdered millions more. America is the only country in the history of the world that has not expanded its territory by acts of offensive aggression. America bought and paid for lands that expanded the size of the US. The one exception was the confiscation of the lands of the First Nation. (The American Indians).

All those nations that committed offensive aggression did so in violation of Natural Law Private Property Rights. Did Hitler throw the first punch? How about Mussolini? North Korea attacked South Korea. Mao Tse-tung and his forces killed all of the landowners, just like the Russian Communists who did the same thing. This was the most efficient way to bring about socialistic land reform.

The only way that collectivization can be accomplished is by the complete denial of private property accompanied by a total loss of freedom. The trend has started in America. Millions believe that God will be our salvation. Unfortunately, if one tried to convince others of this, they would immediately turn you off. On the other hand, if one asks someone if they believe they are poorer because of the political intervention in their affairs, the answer would be, yes. This gives one an opening. One should not attempt to educate to the point of boredom.

Social Interventionists

CHAPTER XI

Not even God would be a social interventionist for He would have to violate His own laws of creation, i.e., the creation of humans with freewill. Scholars debate whether humans have freewill or not. They go on at great length in an attempt to establish that their theories are the only ones that are correct. That is fine for academics; however, for the individual, all one has to know is that one can choose what one will do with his own life.

One is free to choose one's actions time and time again. What more does one need to observe to realize that one has freewill?

There are those who will argue that other creatures are free to choose their actions. Yes, but their actions are limited to constructive actions that promote their survival. Humans are free to choose between creative actions and/or destructive actions. As a layperson, this is all one must know to realize the existence of freewill in humans and why, compared to other creatures, the human mind is corrupt.

Did humans evolve through Nature? If so, why give us freewill and not give it to the other creatures? That would not be possible, for Nature is without intelligence. Even though Nature is without intelligence, Nature created intelligence! I seem to be contradicting myself, but I am not. All of the Laws of Nature exist. Many have not been discovered as yet. Nature is not the creator of God, nor is God the creator of Nature -- because both are infinite. They are without beginning or end!

In the controversy over evolution and creationism, evolution is an act of Nature/God for He created the conditions that made evolution possible. (This is the teaching of Catholicism.) On the other hand, evolution is an act of Nature. Thomas Paine believed that Nature is God (Deism). The Declaration of Independence is a deistic document -- "...the Laws of Nature and Nature's God." (Note that the word "Nature" is in the possessive tense.) According to the founding fathers, God is a possession of Nature. Nature is without beginning or end, and God is without beginning or end. Nature is perfect, and so is God. God is infinite consciousness. Nature never makes a mistake. We are told God is everywhere and sees all things. This has to be accepted as an article of faith. We know Nature is everywhere and acts on all things because we can see Nature at work. In seeing Nature are we seeing God?

*****

Can the acts of the interventionists be recognized as intelligence? How can anyone who is so ignorant as to believe that they have the skill to manage the lives of millions of people who they do not even know, be considered intelligent? They probably cannot even manage their own families!

Government collects endless amounts of statistics. It is necessary so they can manage the many facets of the nation's work. Individuals have no need for statistics to manage their affairs. They make a decision to solve a problem in their personal lives, and then they execute it.

Government is attempting to save the right whale from extinction. A plan to accomplish this has been in the works for eight years. It will be a minimum of five more years before their efforts are complete and become law.

The right whale is the dumbest animal on land or sea. Freighters kill most of the right whales. When a vessel bears down on them, they stay put and make no effort to get out of the way. The humpback and minke whales frequent the same space and seldom, if ever, are run down. The humpback and minke whales also frequent the waters where the lobstermen and gill-netters fish with no problems. We are told that fishing gear is a threat to all species of whales and that many have been found entangled in pot warp (rope). When the head of the Massachusetts Lobstermen's Association investigated, he was refused the opportunity to view the pot warp. When he gave up and was about to leave the building, a custodian directed him to where the pot warp was stored. He followed instructions and found the rope. It was not pot warp but heavy line that must have been thrown overboard from a freighter, or the like.

*****

The job of political interventionists is to change human behavior to conform to the thinking of reformists. The reformists come in all shapes and colors. If a reformist's plan is harmful to America, one can be sure it will be implemented. The reformists have one thing in common -- they are all anti-capitalists, particularly the greens.

Their vision is one where political professionals would manage all aspects of life. Parents are not competent to raise their children. We read about it all the time, and then are reminded on TV. It is our super-corrupt educational system that is never at fault. It is the parents' lack of interest in their children. Although the NEA complains that the shortcomings of education are due to low pay, in the next breath they, again, blame the parents. The parents cannot defend themselves because the media coverage ignores them.

It is said that there are no atheists in foxholes. The soldier prays to survive another day. In many cities the teachers do the same. Corrupt schools, for corrupt minds. "Oh, what fools we mortals be."

*****

The war on terror is the first of its kind in history. The invasion of America has happened before, but not in the form that is coming from Mexico. The invaders do not carry guns! They cross our borders by the thousands. They now number ten to fifteen million. They will soon be the majority in many communities. They will vote their own to rule. At this point there will be nothing that Americans will be able to do to take back control of their towns because they will be a voting minority. Then will come the legalized plunder of the white and black minority. Private property rights will be history. This will all be due to a feckless Congress that puts itself ahead of the welfare of the nation.

The political interventionists will thrive as never before. Their numbers will explode. We will become like India before the reforms when the bureaucrats outnumbered the private sector.

*****

Science is the art of measuring and observing -- things like an atom, the distance to the sun and stars, and the speed of sound and light. Science also studies and observes Nature. Maybe a lot of the political confusion today is due to the fact that our colleges teach political science. What kind of instrument does one use to measure politics? Where does one find consistency in politics? Politics might be an art, but it is not a science.

The private sector scientists look into their microscopes to discover Nature's secrets. They replicate under controlled circumstances the actions of Nature. They study why a machine part failed, and then build a better model. They are disciplined. They do not violate any of Nature's rules. They know that if they do not observe the Laws of Nature, the results of their experiments will be corrupt and meaningless. Yet the loudest voices that deny Natural Law Private Property Rights come from academia.

If the public sector had the discipline of the private sector in all of the nations of the world, the whole world would prosper. All would be well fed, housed, and clothed.

In most of the world, the right to life is not acknowledged. In Africa and Iraq, murder is the national pastime. No one even has a clue as to what private property rights mean. "Ignorance is bliss." "What one does not know, will not hurt him." Where did that nonsense come from? It must have come from Washington.

The tail is wagging the dog. Political interventionists have more power than the president, his cabinet, or the head of the many departments appointed by the president. Harry Truman was outraged when low-level clerks overruled him, and he then found that there was nothing that he could do about it. Laws are passed. The enforcers of these laws ignore the intent of the laws, and enforce the letter of the laws.

The twenty-five mile speed limit is an example. The intent of the law was public safety in the days of the Model-T with its mechanical brakes that worked as well as dragging one's feet on the roadway. The modern auto can stop nearly within its own length at twenty-five miles per hour. The original intent of the law is ignored, but the limit is enforced to this day. "Strictly enforced," the sign reads in many places.

The anti-democracy interventionists are a greater burden on citizens with each passing day. The self-employed, which numbers in the hundreds of thousands, have to save every receipt, regardless of how insignificant it is, if they are to use it as a deduction. Every dollar one spends for which a receipt cannot be produced raises the cost of a purchase by fifteen-percent self-employment tax plus another fifteen-to-twenty-five percent income tax. There are logbooks that follow these reports and paperwork with which one must comply. All are time-consuming and frustrating after a hard day at work. It is the pressure of having to have the reports in on time that is the worst and is damaging to one's health. So why do people comply? -- because of licenses. The penalty for noncompliance with government regulations is the loss of one's license to operate a commercial vessel, work as a carpenter, plumber, truck driver, contractor, etc. When all is said and done, one finds oneself with a loss of freedom and property. The larger the enterprise, the more the cost for extra personnel to keep up with the required red tape. All of the hours used by the private sector to conform to government regulations are hours not spent producing goods and services such as banking, health care, dry-cleaning, car washing, etc.

The same can be said for all government employees who are required to process the endless paper trail. There is a huge workforce that works hard like a car that is stuck in the snow with its wheels spinning a mile a minute and going nowhere.

When a private-sector company finds itself in financial difficulty, it reduces its workforce. The laid-off employees find work where there is a greater need for them. In this way the private sector becomes more efficient. Government never lays off anybody. It does not have to make a profit. It adds employees and becomes less efficient. With another layer of bureaucracy, it will now take three months to do what previously took two. In the private sector, a situation that requires attention will be analyzed and resolved within days. There will be one to a dozen people involved, depending on the size of the business. If the solution proposed turns into a disaster, workers will be replaced, not promoted as with government agencies.

Nature's Laws of Mechanics

CHAPTER XII

To build a machine, one must follow the Laws of Nature step by step without question. From the mining of the ore, to the mill and from the shaping of the steel, to the castings and finally to the finished product, Nature is the boss.

Mechanics is a complex and many-sided subject. My purpose for presenting it here is to demonstrate the complete dependence on Natural Law that this discipline requires. All the sciences are referred to as *disciplines* because they demand strict obedience and compliance to Natural Law. The contrasts between the actions of scientists and those of government are startling.

Everything from the atom bomb to the changing of a tire is part of the science of mechanics. It is the branch of physics that is concerned with the motion of physical objects and the forces that cause or limit these motions.

"Mechanics can be seen as the prime, and even the original, discipline of physics. It is a huge body of knowledge about the natural world." "Mechanics also constitutes a central part of technology. That is: how to apply this knowledge for humanly defined purposes. In this connection, the discipline is often known as engineering mechanics or applied mechanics." (Wikipedia)

Mechanics deals with truth as it exists in Nature. The search for these truths is never-ending. New truths are discovered every day. In the field of electronics, it is difficult to keep up with the advances in technology. The wheelhouse in a commercial fishing vessel is beginning to look like the interior of a spacecraft with all of its electronic devices. Technology has made the commercial fishing vessel efficient to the point that it threatens the resource. This is the excuse that the greens and political interventionists are using to descend on the industry in hoards. They are regulating it to death.

If regulators stayed out of the way, the less efficient would go out of business as the stocks were depleted. The pressure of over-fishing would take care of itself. Eventually, the stocks would recover and the pressure would once again mount. Like the deer in the forest, as their numbers flourish because of an abundance of food, so then they diminish when overgrazing takes place. The process occurs over and over again.

The point that needs to be clearly understood is the great efficiency of scientists, compared to the bungling of bureaucrats. We can marvel at the wonders that Nature brings to us through the efforts of scientists as we despair over the antics of the state. The scientists never stop searching. The politicians never stop talking. The scientists want truth. The politicians want power.

The majority must demand that the politicians serve the community as the scientists serve the world. The politician must devote himself to the principles of Natural Law in his efforts to serve the nation. He must limit himself, as the scientist limits himself, in his never-ending search for the truth.

Some good places to start clearing the political maggot heaps would be to do away with the UN, the World Bank, the European Union, and any other organization that claims authority over more than one nation.

The false premise is that big is better and bigger is even better. Actually, big is corrupt and bigger is more corrupt. It is inevitable that the sun will rise every morning. It is inevitable that politicians will be corrupted every day. The founders of the American Nation knew this. They sought to severely limit the power of the central government. The powers that they did not specifically enumerate to the central government were given to the states and the people therein. They knew that to limit abuse, they must give power to the smallest unit of government.

The principles of subsidiary suggest that the smallest unit of government that is capable of performing a function should control that function. On the community level, for instance, the community is capable of providing fire protection; therefore, that function should be limited to community control. The local community can adequately provide education; therefore, its function should be controlled by the local school board.

The individual states should regulate highways, National Guard, rivers, inshore ocean fishing, and other functions that it can perform, but the individual towns cannot. The federal government has the duty to regulate money, the post office, national defense, and international treaties. These functions are beyond the ability of cities and states.

This discussion must turn to the mechanics of industrial economics. It is here that all the flaws of modern economics lie. Flawed economics result in individual loss of property rights. It is worth repeating. It is not necessary that the layperson understand the sophistication of the many economic theories. One must understand that his wages are his to spend as he pleases. No one in his or her right mind will deny that. It is when one argues that the right of the individual to spend his money as he pleases is capitalism that we run into doublethink. The proponents of legalized plunder are excellent at convincing the electorate that their [opinions] will be to the voters gain because someone else will pay their benefits.

One has to wonder why the politicians spend many times more money to get elected than what they will be paid if elected. The answer is their salary is but a small part of their income. For example, they pay nothing into Social Security; but when they retire, it is at full pay. Add to this other perks that can amount to millions, such as the privilege to keep their campaign funds when they retire. And one must not lose sight of the ego trip of holding public office and "serving their constituents".

Bill and Hillary Clinton took a fortune of historic furnishings when Bill left office. This is but one example of the crimes committed by our "public servants" that never are prosecuted. Politicians never prosecute politicians, except in rare cases. After all, it is called the free market. They grab the free and ignore the market.

*****

I attended a function many years ago at Philips Exeter Academy in New Hampshire where Bill Buckley was the speaker. At the close of the speech he had a Q&A. A female student argued with Buckley in an attempt to make him look like a fool by asking several simple questions. Buckley ended the harassment by saying, "We take for granted that people of normal intelligence are capable of making simple distinctions."

I had a similar experience after giving a talk on Natural Law Private Property Rights. An audience member turned the discussion to claiming that the confiscation of the Cuban citizens' property meant that the property was now Castro's private property. Buckley's answer to the student served me well in making a fool look like a fool.

It is difficult to understand how error in the mechanics of economics is widely held, when the truth is obvious. Is the overwhelming majority's inability to make simple distinctions the cause? Or is it the incompetence of those who advocate Natural Law Private Property Rights? I ask myself what am I doing writing this essay when men of great genius have made the arguments before me and some are still around today? Why is it that capitalism is not understood when it has been explained by people like Adam Smith. Frederic Bastiat, Philip Wicksteed, Ludwig von Mises, Henry Hazlitt, Leonard Read, James A. Donald, and several others?

The true supporter of private property is one who sees the corruption of humans and is determined to reform humankind by starting with oneself. As I have said before, "Everyone wants to reform the world, but no one will help mama with the dishes." As pure as I think of myself to be, I cash my Social Security check every month.

I am proud of an incident I had with the VA. I went to apply for my ID. I wanted to get my meds at a substantial discount. I did not realize that a mental health worker was interviewing me. I was stunned by the insight of the interviewer. A few minutes into the interview I realized that she knew more about me, than I. As the interview went on, she insisted that I apply for disability. I refused. She argued that I had fought for our country. Still I refused. In exasperation she said that I deserved my reward. At that point I told her I had my reward, I was born an American! I still have not used my ID, nor will I ever. And I am going to stop cashing my Social Security check as soon as I die!

I raced stock cars in Louden, NH, for several years. One can observe the Natural Laws of Mechanics as a spectator or a crewmember on a racing team. The engine of the car has to be built to perfection, or it will explode before the race is over. The same can be said for the drivetrain. The tire construction is a science in itself. To build and drive a stock car requires experts in ten to twenty of the Natural sciences. To find the best groove in a racetrack is a skill held by few drivers. Every track has its top ten, and every week they are the ones up front. They know the exact speed to enter a curve without losing traction. If you go a mile or two over the optimum speed, the car will crash. NASCAR fans can tell with near certainty who will be in the top five and top ten every week.

It is like commercial fishing. The captain who understands the art of the fishery in which he operates will be the highliner year after year. The best deckhands will seek to become crewmembers under his supervision.

The captains are intimate with Nature. They work with Her. Never will they fight Nature or take their eyes from Her. They can look at Her through the wheelhouse window and tell whether She is in a good mood or about to start kicking ass.

*****

What a friend we have in science. Unless it is junk science that we fall prey to. Rachel Carson's *Silent Spring* is junk science. In nineteen forty in India, seventy-five million people fell ill from malaria; eight hundred thousand people died every year. By nineteen sixty, DDT had reduced the number of victims to less than fifty thousand. In Sri Lanka, DDT was started in nineteen forty-six. Eighteen years later, the victim count had gone from three million to TWENTY-NINE! -- that's 29!

Today DDT is banned once more. Death from malaria is back where it was before DDT was used the first time. The tragic part is that it is the children who are dying in great numbers! Due to that fact, many communities are defying the ban.

Junk science was used to save the spotted owl in the Northwest. It destroyed the northwest lumber industry and the thousands of families who depended on it for their livelihood. It has since been found that the forest industry had no bearing on the population of the spotted owl.

I have already covered the damage being done in the northeast by junk science. The excuse is that the millions of dollars being spent by the fishermen to comply with the regulations to make the fishing gear whale-safe will save the right whale from extinction. It is the northeast's spotted owl fiasco.

Those who finance the greens can best be known by seeing who is paying their bills? -- billionaires such as George Soros, for example. How can people who are without gainful employment travel the world over to raise havoc against capitalism? How can Green Peace maintain a navy to disrupt fishing all over the world? Of course, those who have made fortunes by taking advantage of capitalistic systems finance them.

Unfortunately, people with half a brain are violating Nature's Laws of Mechanics. It is frightening to see the consequences of freewill. Is freewill a good thing? Is it freewill that brings about the loss of property rights, and the choice of drugs, rather than sanity? Is it freewill that brings about the gangs here in America and the terrorists here and throughout the world? Is the murder and mayhem everywhere, and the wars without end brought about because of freewill?

Is it freewill that is the cause of great humanitarian deeds and the endless search for truth and the secrets of Nature that benefits all of humanity? Is it freewill that causes us to appreciate the endless beauty of truth and Nature?

Obedience

CHAPTER XIII

There is no question that Nature must be obeyed in manufacturing, farming, forestry, fishing, etc., because the results of failing to do so are obvious.

In the hills of Kentucky a county agricultural agent explained to a farmer that he should plow his land along the contour of the grade rather than up and down the elevation. The agent explained that contour plowing would substantially reduce the erosion of the topsoil. The farmer became indignant. He told the agricultural agent, "Don't try and tell me how to farm. I've already worn out four farms."

A Maine farmer visited some farms in Texas. At one farm he was asked how many acres he worked.

"About two hundred," he replied.

"Is that all?" the Texan asked.

"Why I can get in my pickup at daybreak and drive all day and still not make it all the way around my farm," the Texan boasted.

"A-yuh," the Mainer replied. "Had a truck like that myself once."

At a time when the country was suffering from the worst drought that anyone had ever experienced, a county agricultural agent addressed a large gathering of Texas farmers at the grange hall. He explained how the government was going to build a twenty-foot-diameter water main from the Great Lakes to the Texas border. At the border the pipe would be reduced from twenty feet to a half inch. The audience gasped.

"Why reduce it to a half inch at our border?" they asked.

"Because," the agent explained, "if you Texans can suck half as good as you can blow, you will have all the water you need."

"There are none so blind as those who refuse to see." This type of blindness is a worldwide epidemic. As the farmers mentioned above, one can see the size of the task. With the mainstream-media monopoly in steady decline, there is hope that the obvious will become apparent. Nature is a dictator. It demands strict obedience. It is judge and jury. There is no way to appeal its punishment. It is weird to think of Nature as a ruler when it is without intelligence. All Laws of Nature are superior to any manmade laws, and such laws come into being by "intelligent" people.

I was asked by the school board of the town of Alton, NH, to present arguments to the superintendent. The subject was sex education that was being presented. The school board believed that the way the subject was being taught was more for the titillating pleasure of the teachers rather than for the education of the students.

The debate went on for about twenty minutes when the superintendent attempted to end it by saying, "Ben

Franklin said that a little knowledge is dangerous." To which I replied that if he were making the same statement today, he would say that a little knowledge is dangerous; but a great deal of knowledge, without wisdom, is far more dangerous. That was the end of the discussion. Ben Franklin never made that statement. It was a Franciscan priest in the nineteenth century whose name escapes me.

Once again the human mind is found to be flawed. What would be the state of humankind if humans had the same intelligence that they now possess, but did not have freewill? Like all other creatures, they would be denied the ability to violate Nature. It is curiosity that drives us to search for Nature's truths. Freewill has little to do with it. The scientist goes from step "A", to "B", to "C', etc. He follows the lead that the different stages of his research lead him. He/she is completely obedient to the direction that the findings dictate. It is intelligence that makes it possible to discover hidden scientific truths. Freewill is not in the equation! Freewill is the first cause of mischief among humans. It is the cause of dysfunctional families to the worst mischief of all, wars.

If you disregard freewill, the Laws of God and Nature are strikingly similar. All would be obedient. Tools that lighten workloads are a demonstration of intelligence, not of freewill. The great apes use tools along with other primates. They do not possess freewill. All creatures acquire knowledge and demonstrate intelligence, but not freewill.

God and Nature are like vines, interwound, reaching skyward. I keep telling my wife that we live in heaven. The forest surrounds our home. At the moment, the clean, fresh green of spring is everywhere we look. There are no neighbors visible other than the creatures of the forest. We have an abundance of them. When we step out the door, they will run to us and beg for peanuts. They are the reason that I believe they are intelligent and have a capacity to learn.

It is little wonder that humans move through life in mass confusion. There is not a word or concept that academics, through their power of reasoning and rationalization, cannot interpret until one is in a total state of confusion. This is not a reflection on laypeople. Academics, themselves, cannot agree on much of anything. This is understandable. Unlike the scientist who is limited to going from one deciphered truth to the next, the philosophers are going from one perceived truth (opinion) to another. Quite often the philosopher's truth is nothing more than an educated opinion.

I will repeat what I have already said -- it is not necessary for the layperson to be familiar with the sophistication of the academics. One must be familiar with this basic truth -- THE MONEY IN YOUR POCKET IS YOURS! Anyone who takes it from you infringes on your Natural Law Private Property Rights and, consequently, your right to life. This can be done in one of two ways, through legalized plunder, i.e., government, or through illegal plunder, i.e., thieves, scam artists, etc.

Experiments have been done to demonstrate how people can be turned into puppets. The Hitler youth movement was successful in turning the youth of Germany into adults who would automatically obey orders, no matter how outrageous.

Military personnel are trained to take orders many times over until they are at the point where they automatically obey commands without question. At Paris Island, during World War II, a troop of recruits marched into the ocean where several drowned because no one gave the order to halt. Close-order drill is where one learns to obey commands without thought.

The same happens on commercial fishing vessels. The captain is not to be trifled with. An order must be obeyed instantly. It could very well be a matter of life and death. A boss onshore does not command instant obedience. The individual being ordered about can walk off the job. That alternative does not exist at sea. A captain can still hang a person for mutiny or insubordination. Before a situation would deteriorate to that extreme, the offending individual would be put in restraints, or shot, if he posed a threat to the vessel and crew.

*****

One obeys the demands that one's body makes for food, sleep, sex, bladder, and bowel relief. These are needs that cannot be ignored. The less obvious demands of Nature can be ignored or violated.

Nature demands obedience. One cannot walk on the bottom of the sea without drowning. Government demands obedience to its rules and regulations, guidelines and laws. Agents are everywhere – the political mosquitoes that swarm over the body of economics. Unfortunately, they do not disappear when the cold weather arrives.

Like a nagging person, one has to be constantly alert while driving to make sure that one is in compliance with the latest government mandate. "Click it, or ticket." We are free, but for how much longer. There is an atmosphere of fear and outrage. People are unsure of the future. The middle-aged people are not all that concerned about their freedom. Their grandchildren are the cause of their concern. What sort of life will they have as the heavy hand of government is laid upon them? At the moment, they see the taxes on their homes doubling and tripling! Although, they see the possibility of losing their homes to the tax person, not an unfounded fear since it has happened before; it is their grandchildren's futures that cause the greatest anxiety. In many fishing families, the parents insist that their college-aged children get an education before they join the crew on a fishing boat.

The backbone of Maine's economy is fishing. The coastline is dotted with fishing villages. However, there are no fishermen living in these villages. Like myself, they have moved into undeveloped places. The people from away are now after our homes in the forest. The taxes on these properties in the evaluations that are being done will increase fifty percent to one hundred percent. On my home, the taxes have increased one hundred sixty percent in twenty-five years. I will be forced to move again. Like it, or not, my friends and I will be driven out. The culture that we constitute and the minor nation that we comprise will be destroyed. Individuals who know nothing about our culture will replace us; and they, in turn, will be evicted after a couple more state-mandated re-evaluations. The government will have to print another bunch of money before that happens. Webster defines inflation as the government inflating the money supply. Why is the worker always blamed?

We must obey the state. They are the ones who carry the guns. The authorities who stand over us represent force and liberty. Gradually, as our liberty is eroded, force will be the only thing left.

As we are forced to obey the regulations of government, life will become more difficult as we struggle to understand the many regulations that we will be compelled to obey.

Even those who live below the poverty level have to go to professionals to file their IRS taxes. Major corporations now have resident IRS agents on their premises full time. GE's last tax return was comprised of over one-and-a-half thousand pages!

The other side of the coin is that all must obey Natural Law. Natural Law is solid. It is not vague. It is constant. There are no amendments attached to it. It does not require huge appropriation bills. There are not several levels of bureaucracy over Natural Law before effect follows cause. There are no gun-toting enforcers following us around to pounce on us should we deviate from the dictated course.

We stand before Nature as we stand before God, with a pure conscience that can see all we have done in our lifetimes. We will pass judgment on ourselves. We will see obedience as we see and feel the sun on a clear day. We will be as calm as the ocean on a windless day. There will be no noise pollution. Traffic noises from the land and the sky will no longer do violence to our sense of hearing. We will enjoy perfect peace in Nature's womb where life begins and ends. Here we will be at peace.

The imperfection of our minds will be history. As the centuries roll by, they will have no effect on us. Throughout life we struggled. In school we suffered the abuses of bullies. Then there were the indignities of straw bosses. There was marriage and the raising of a family. There was the joy when family members were good and the pain when they were not. The constant fights to meet financial responsibilities. The stress of never having enough income.

Then comes failing health and strength. As the end appears nearer and nearer, obedience becomes easier. Realization strikes like thunder. Now is the time to live in all of the wonderful memories. When the end arrives, there will be no problems. There will be only peace.

Debate

CHAPTER XIV

Debate rages without end in politics and economics. Assuming the debaters are honest, informed, and objective, how can this be? After considerable thought, I realize that the combination of honesty and objectivity does not exist in the political arena. Opinion rules the day.

There are many outside the political arena who are capable of honesty and objectivity, but do not look to the mainstream media for answers. Anyone who has read this far knows where to find reliable information and opinion.

Debate is vital. It is through debate that knowledge is advanced. Debate is the art of persuasion. To reform society one must limit oneself to persuasion. Force has no place in debates; it is the antithesis of persuasion and freedom. Debate is the friend of freedom. Dictators do not permit debate.

It was debate that produced the Declaration of Independence and the Constitution. Debate brought about the Civil War and every war in which America has been involved. They were all wars of self-defense -- America committed defensive violence in the name of self-preservation.

In a debate one participant can be wrong, and the other right. Both participants can be wrong. Never can both participants, who hold opposite points of view, be right.

Debate is the prime mover in all government action. Private property rights have been dealt a crushing blow because of arguments presented to the Supreme Court. The court ruling has sparked an enthusiastic debate regarding citizens' rights to private property. The *Kelo v. City of New London* ruling has set off an alarm throughout the country as to how delicate our rights are. People are outraged. In a letter to me, Senior Senator of Maine, Olympia Snowe, wrote, "You expressed concern with a Supreme Court ruling that occurred on June 23, 2005. As you know the court ruled 5-4 in *Kelo v. City of New London*, that a Connecticut town would exercise its power of eminent domain under a state law to force several homeowners to vacate their properties so that it could be used for private commercial development. I find this decision particularly alarming due to the fact that protection of homes, small business, and other private property rights against government seizure and other unreasonable government interference is a fundamental principle and core commitment of our founding fathers. The Fifth Amendment of the United States Constitution guarantees that private property shall not be taken for public use without just compensation. The Fifth Amendment thus provides an essential guarantee of liberty against the abuse of power of eminent domain. By permitting government to seize private property **only for public use.**" (Emphasis the Senator)

"Therefore I have joined several colleagues in co-sponsoring a bill introduced by Senator John Cornyn, S.1313, The Protection *of Homes, Small Business, and Private Property Act.* This bill will bar state and local government from using federal funds for economic development that involves exercising eminent domain. Upon introduction, S 1313 was referred to the Senate Judiciary Committee for review. The committee held hearings on the bill on September 20, 2005. At this time, there is no indication of when the bill will be marked up before the committee. Should this or similar legislation come under consideration of the full Senate, please be assured that I will keep your thoughts in mind." Signed Senator Olympia Snowe.

Should it be necessary to debate the right to private property after two hundred years of successful capitalism? At present the anti-capitalists are winning the debate. They have won a huge victory in *Kelo v. City of New London.* A victory equal to *Roe v. Wade* by the advocates of legalized abortion. Abortion is legal. Prostitution is a crime! There is something wrong with that picture.

The Supreme Court has taken it upon itself to study foreign laws to aid it in its deliberation. Eminent domain proceedings are more liberal in Europe. The interpretation of eminent domain limited to the taking of private property for public use now includes commercial use. As such, no one's property is safe.

There are just laws, not necessarily based on Natural Law that must be obeyed. To determine if a law is just, ask yourself, "Does it fend off or stop destructive actions?" An unjust law is one that interferes with the creative actions of citizens.

The burden of compliance grows and grows. Time is lost from productive work. Time is lost on paperwork with the threat of several times the paper load of today, in the near future. Thank God and Bill Gates for the computer, or we would be using all of our waking hours at the kitchen table drinking coffee and working on paperwork to keep the government up-to-date on our activities.

The private sector is hard at work, obeying the laws applicable to their particular specialty, to produce new and better products. Up goes productivity. Soon everybody will be enjoying the latest widget.

As government swarms over the private sector, it produces another horde of mosquitoes to drive everyone to distraction.

One could go so far as to say that Nature is democratic. If the majority of the citizens in a nation understand Natural Law Private Property Rights, they will then elect people who believe as they do. Under these circumstances, even those who are not familiar with Natural Law, or do not agree, will benefit from the results of peace and prosperity.

Obedience to Natural Law brings about immediate rewards. Obedience to the Commandments will be rewarded after death. Actually the parallels between Natural Law and the Commandments bring about the same results. In a democratic nation, it is essential that the rule of Nature or God guide the majority -- one or the other. There is no other way to eliminate poverty. Government must be bound by Natural Law. Only by a clear understanding of the principles of Natural Law can one judge those who would impose their will on the nation.

The view through the eyes of Nature is like looking through a clean pair of glasses. It is a joy to be able to see through so much of the nonsense that passes as wisdom.

Natural Law vs. Opinion

To repeat what I said earlier, abortion is legal, but prostitution is a crime. Those who agree with the above statement do so on the basis of their opinions. Those who disagree, do so based on their opinions. Through the eyes of Nature we see that abortion is a violation of the Laws of Nature because what is being aborted is the next generation that will contribute to the survival of the human species.

The unknown here is whether the earth has reached its capacity to support the human species? If it hasn't, then will it ever; and if it does, will population control be the only way to save our species from extinction? Under those circumstances will abortion conform to the Laws of Nature?

Sex between married couples, unmarried couples, or with a prostitute is in compliance with the authority of the Laws of Nature because the act could result in pregnancy. Prostitution is not a violation of Natural Law; therefore, it is not a crime, but abortion is.

One can look at gay marriage the same way. Those who favor gay marriage do so based on their opinions. Those who oppose it, do so based on their opinions. Sex between two men or two women is a violation of Natural Law because procreation is not possible. That is obvious.

Violations of Natural Law Private Property Rights will bring about poverty just as sure as gay sex will not produce children, nor will it contribute to the health of the human species.

What one must understand is that the Laws of Nature rule and must be obeyed. Whereas laws based on the authority of governments are opinions and must be scrutinized to be in compliance with Natural Law. If they are not in agreement with Natural Law, they are destructive in nature and must be abolished. If they are constructive, they deserve the support of the governed.

Poverty is not caused by a violation of God's Laws. Poverty is caused by the violations of Nature's Laws.

Governments do not deny private property rights in the name of God, but in the name of "progress" which results in a violation of Natural Law Private Property Rights. By denying private property rights in the name of progress, governments create poverty.

Natural Law preceded the Commandments, therefore, preceded Divine Law. The Laws of God, as expressed in the Bible, apply only to humans. Natural Law applies to all living creatures and to all inanimate objects. The Grand Canyon was created by Nature by the process of erosion. God did not create it. Therefore, is Natural Law more inclusive than Divine Law?

Humans are subject to Divine Law and to Natural Law. All other creatures are subject to Natural Law only. No wonder we humans are so screwed up.

It is incumbent upon all of the friends of freedom that they be familiar with Natural Law -- i.e., the income that the worker generates belongs to the worker, and to no one else!

He is free to delegate his right to self-defense to his government whose duty it is to protect him from all that would do him harm. Taxes that make it possible for the government to do its duty are just. Anything beyond that is legalized plunder.

The right sees the power and beauty of Nature and God. It has developed a rational hate of the left because it threatens the wellbeing of those on the right.

The left sees the "truths" that the right represents and has developed an irrational hate of the right and of the truths that it advocates. The left is offensive action, and the right is defensive action. (Erich Fromm, *The Art of Loving*)

The greens scream that human action is damaging the planet. They do not realize that their arguments are based on a twisted understanding of Natural Law.

Actually, they come to their conclusions by limiting themselves to the acts of humans. To them, humans cause storms, erosion, earthquakes, global warming, etc.

Offensive acts are a violation of Natural Law. Defensive acts are mandated by Natural Law.

Because Divine Law applies only to humans, The Commandments did not apply prior to the existence of man. Natural Law has existed forever, and it applies to all things.

Nature and God are without beginning and without end, so one could not have created the other.

A few thousand years ago, God gave The Commandments to Moses. They are as relevant today, as they were then. Take a look at them. Is there anything you would change?

The Constitution was written two hundred years ago. Just as The Commandments are relevant today, so is the Constitution. The call for a "living" Constitution is nonsense. The Constitution and The Commandments will be as relevant a thousand years from today, as they are now. Morality does not change with the advancement of technology.

*****

You cannot solve a mathematical problem by the use of only half of the applicable formula. By the same token, we cannot solve our social problems by the use of only half of the formula advanced by the founders. It is stated in the Declaration of Independence that we are entitled to the protection of the "Laws of Nature and Nature's God".

Those in the forefront of the fight for our rights argue that our rights come from God. They are only half-right. It is half the formula. They neglect to argue the authority of the Laws of Nature. You cannot solve a mathematical problem by the use of half of the formula. We cannot solve our social problems by the use of half of the formula upon which the success of this nation was built.

If governments were limited to the protection of the citizens' rights to life, freedom, and the income from their labor, they would function within the "Laws of Nature and Nature's God". If governments maintained this ideal condition, they could then get out of our way.

The BP oil spill is a good example of how the government has not responded, as it should have. They, then, got in the way of the private citizens' efforts to solve the problem. With this oil crisis, Obama and his people are like a fire crew having responded to a building fire, with the building entirely engulfed, and then their having to wait for an EPA study before they can put out the fire!

*****

The person who does not believe in the "Laws of Nature and Nature's God" is a person without direction. Like a ship that is disabled at sea and has lost its anchor, he is lost and has no control over where he will end up.

His mind will fire in all *directions*. His opinions will have no foundation in *truth*.

THE END

Suggested reading:

Brendan Brown - *The Natural Law Reader*

Charles Garnache - *Nature, The Lobsterman's Master and Poverty, a Violation of Law*

F.A. Hayek - *The Road to Serfdom*

Henry Hazlitt - *Economics in One Lesson*

Natural Law on Wikipedia - One will find that the simple premise, the worker's wages belong to the worker, can be rationalized to death.

Leonard Read - Any of his thirty manuscripts.

Henry Hazlitt has compiled a list of 550 books for the serious student of economics and freedom. They range from books for beginners to books for the most serious of students.